Study, Hustle, Repeat: The H.U.S.T.L.E. Bible Study Method

Copyright 2021

www.HustleGodsWay.com
info@hustlegodsway.com

ISBN: 978-1-7358359-2-1

ALL RIGHTS RESERVED.
No part of this publication may be reproduced, stored, or transmitted in any form or by any means – for example, electronic, photocopy or recording – without prior written permission. The only exception are brief quotations in printed reviews. Please encourage and participate in doing the right thing.

Cover design by The Vision to Fruition Publishing House
(www.vtfpublishing.com)

Printed in the United States of America

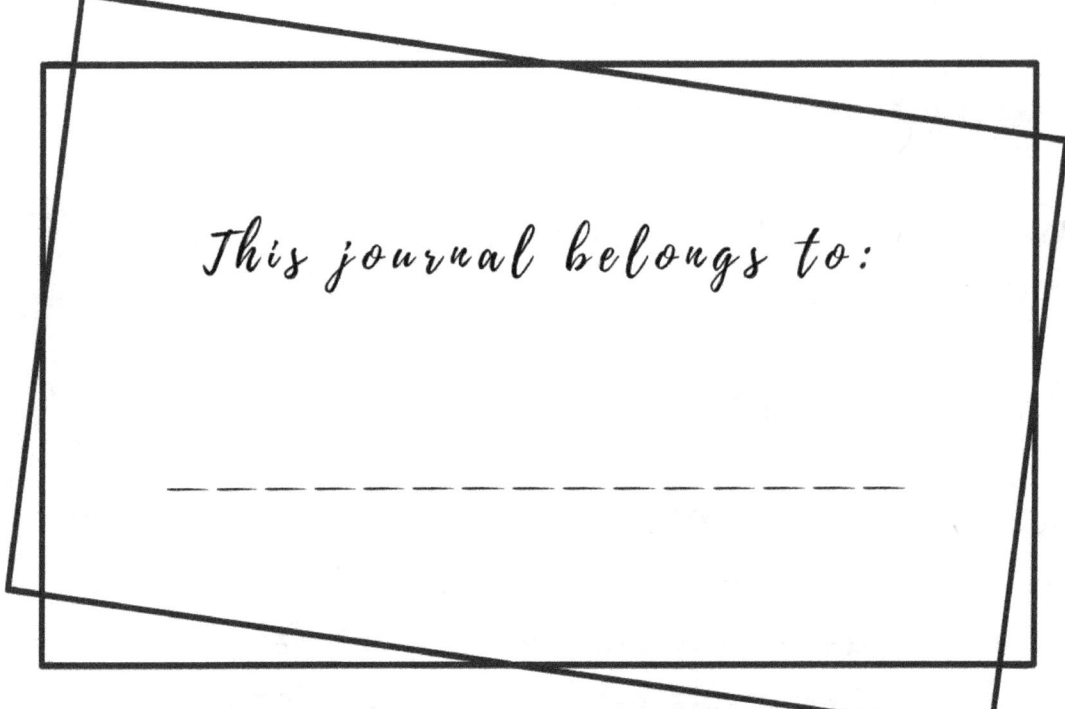

This journal belongs to:

_____

The H.U.S.T.L.E. Bible Study Method

The H.U.S.T.L.E. Bible Study Method

To hustle God's way, we must:

Study His Word Daily

The Bible is an incredible book that proves that there is a God that created all things. Most important of all, the Bible is the Word of God. It contains the mind of God and His will for each one of our lives. That is why the Bible was given to us. The Apostle Paul says in 2 Timothy 3:16-17, "All Scripture is given by inspiration of God, and is profitable for doctrine, for reproof, for correction, for instruction in righteousness, that the man of God may be complete, thoroughly equipped for every good work."

"Whether we are reading the Bible for the first time or standing in a field in Israel next to a historian and an archaeologist and a scholar, the Bible meets us where we are. That is what truth does."

Leonard Ravenhill

7 Reasons Why We Should Study the Bible

1. The Bible helps us defeat doubts, fear and anxiety by strengthening our faith.
2. The Bible helps us fight sin in our lives.
3. The Bible helps us to make decisions according to His will so that He will bless us.
4. The Bible helps us stand strong against the crafty schemes of the devil.
5. The Bible helps us to detect error in a world filled with lies.
6. The Bible is powerful enough to revive the soul when you are hurting or discouraged.
7. The Bible helps us to grow in our knowledge of Jesus Christ so that the cravings of our soul may be satisfied.

How to Study the Bible
The H.U.S.T.L.E. Way

H — **HUMBLE**
Humble yourself and pray.

U — **UNDERSTAND**
Look up different translations, definitions and cross references.

S — **STUDY**
What is the text saying to me?

T — **TUNE IN**
Relax, let go, be quiet before the Lord and listen.

L — **LIVE**
How can you apply this Word to your life?

E — **ENCOURAGE**
How I can share what I have learned to help someone else?

The H.U.S.T.L.E. Bible Study Method

Date:

HUMBLE
yourself and pray.

James 1:5, KJV:
"If any of you lack wisdom, let him ask of God, that giveth to all men liberally, and upbraideth not; and it shall be given him."

Lord, thank You for this time You've given me to open Your Word and discover who You are. Thank You that You don't leave us in the dark about who You are and what You are doing in the world, but that You have revealed Yourself and Your Will through the Bible, Your sacred Words to us.

Lord, I need wisdom as I read Your Word. You promise us in James 1:5 that we only have to ask for wisdom to receive it. Lord, please give me Your wisdom now as I approach Your Word. Help me discern the truth of this text. Help me not rely on my own understanding. Thank you God for the clarity, encouragement and hope Your Word brings.

In Jesus' Name I pray, Amen.

Use the space below to pray specifically about what you would like God to reveal through your Bible Study.

Dear Heavenly Father:

_____
_____
_____
_____
_____
_____
_____
_____
_____
_____
_____
_____
_____
_____
_____
_____
_____
_____
_____
_____
_____
_____
_____
_____
_____
_____
_____
_____

In Jesus Name I pray, Amen

UNDERSTAND

Look up different translations, definitions and cross references.

Scripture: _____

Use the space below to write out the scripture in your favorite translation, then choose another translation to write the scripture out.

Favorite Translation:

_____
_____
_____
_____
_____
_____
_____

Another Translation:

_____
_____
_____
_____
_____
_____
_____

Note any words that are different between the two translations. Use a Bible Dictionary to look up the words. Also read the cross-reference scriptures to dive deeper into the scripture and gain a better understanding.

UNDERSTAND

Words that stand out/are different per translation:

_____
_____
_____
_____
_____
_____
_____

Definitions:

_____
_____
_____
_____
_____
_____
_____
_____

Cross-Reference Scriptures:

_____
_____
_____
_____
_____
_____
_____
_____

STUDY
What is the text saying to me?

Use the S.P.E.C.K. Method to explore the text.

S.IN TO CONFESS + AVOID

In the passage, does God say something about sin? Is there a sin to confess? Is there a sin that I should avoid?

P.ROMISE TO KEEP

Does God communicate a promise for me to claim?

E.XAMPLE TO FOLLOW

Do I find role models in this passage? What character traits and which actions are commendable? Which are not?

C.OMMAND TO OBEY

Are there any specific commands given for me to follow. What does God want me to apply to my life today and this week so that I develop Godly character and habits?

K. – KNOWLEDGE ABOUT GOD

What does this passage tell me about God or about Jesus Christ or the Holy Spirit? What is God like? What are His attributes? What does He do? What does He like and dislike? What is His attitude?

NOTE - you can't always answer all 5 parts.

STUDY

S. in to confess + avoid

_____
_____
_____
_____
_____
_____
_____

P. romise to keep

_____
_____
_____
_____
_____
_____
_____

E. xample to follow

_____
_____
_____
_____
_____
_____
_____

STUDY

C. ommand to obey

_____
_____
_____
_____
_____
_____
_____
_____
_____
_____

K. nowledge about God

_____
_____
_____
_____
_____
_____
_____
_____
_____
_____
_____
_____
_____
_____
_____
_____

TUNE IN

Relax, let go, be quiet before the Lord and listen.

This is a time of focus. Focus on the scripture and set your mind on the Father, Son, and Holy Spirit. Take as much time as you need. Don't rush this part! After some time has passed, use the space below to write anything God revealed or spoke to you.

_____
_____
_____
_____
_____
_____
_____
_____
_____
_____
_____
_____
_____
_____
_____
_____
_____
_____
_____
_____
_____
_____
_____
_____
_____

LIVE

How can you apply this Word to your life?

Why does what I learned today matter? How do I implement it in my life today? How should my perspective change based on what I have learned? Look for applications that affect your relationship to God, with others, and your view of self. Use the space below to explore these questions.

_____

ENCOURAGE

How I can share what I have learned to help someone else?

When do I plan to share this? Who do I plan to sharing this with? How do I plan to share this? In-person? Text message? Phone call? Social Media? Use the space below to develop a plan of action.

_____
_____
_____
_____
_____
_____
_____
_____
_____
_____
_____
_____
_____
_____
_____
_____
_____
_____
_____
_____
_____
_____
_____

Additional Notes:

_____
_____
_____
_____
_____
_____
_____
_____
_____
_____
_____
_____
_____
_____
_____
_____
_____
_____
_____
_____
_____
_____
_____
_____
_____
_____
_____
_____
_____

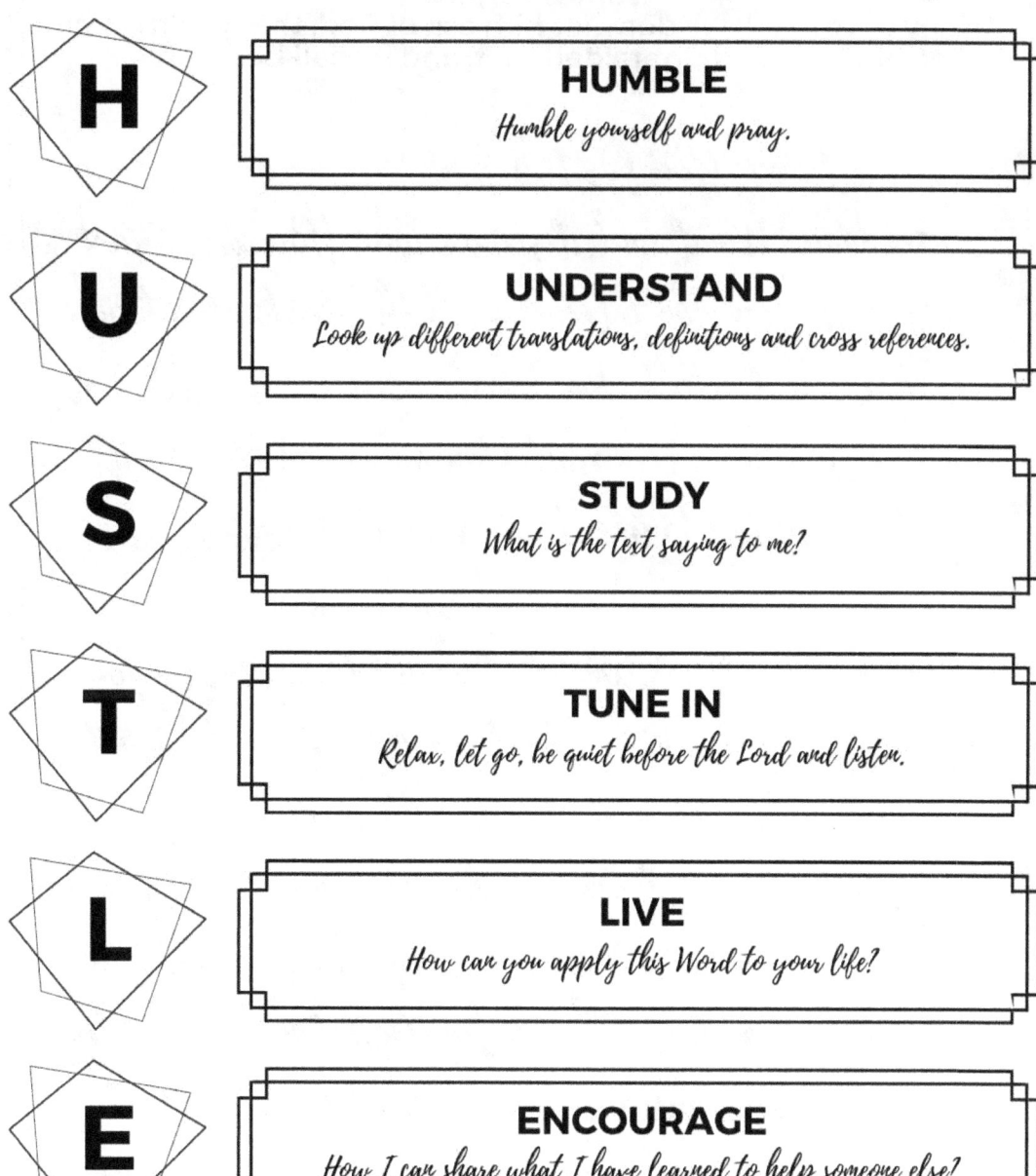

Date:

HUMBLE
yourself and pray.

James 1:5, KJV:
"If any of you lack wisdom, let him ask of God, that giveth to all men liberally, and upbraideth not; and it shall be given him."

Lord, thank You for this time You've given me to open Your Word and discover who You are. Thank You that You don't leave us in the dark about who You are and what You are doing in the world, but that You have revealed Yourself and Your Will through the Bible, Your sacred Words to us.

Lord, I need wisdom as I read Your Word. You promise us in James 1:5 that we only have to ask for wisdom to receive it. Lord, please give me Your wisdom now as I approach Your Word. Help me discern the truth of this text. Help me not rely on my own understanding. Thank you God for the clarity, encouragement and hope Your Word brings.

In Jesus' Name I pray, Amen.

Use the space below to pray specifically about what you would like God to reveal through your Bible Study.

Dear Heavenly Father:

_____
_____
_____
_____
_____
_____
_____
_____
_____
_____
_____
_____
_____
_____
_____
_____
_____
_____
_____
_____
_____
_____
_____
_____
_____
_____
_____
_____
_____
_____
_____
_____

In Jesus Name I pray, Amen

UNDERSTAND

Look up different translations, definitions and cross references.

Scripture: _____

Use the space below to write out the scripture in your favorite translation, then choose another translation to write the scripture out.

Favorite Translation:

_____
_____
_____
_____
_____
_____
_____
_____
_____
_____

Another Translation:

_____
_____
_____
_____
_____
_____
_____
_____
_____
_____

Note any words that are different between the two translations. Use a Bible Dictionary to look up the words. Also read the cross-reference scriptures to dive deeper into the scripture and gain a better understanding.

UNDERSTAND

Words that stand out/are different per translation:

_____
_____
_____
_____
_____
_____
_____

Definitions:

_____
_____
_____
_____
_____
_____
_____

Cross-Reference Scriptures:

_____
_____
_____
_____
_____
_____
_____

STUDY

What is the text saying to me?

Use the S.P.E.C.K. Method to explore the text.

S.IN TO CONFESS + AVOID

In the passage, does God say something about sin? Is there a sin to confess? Is there a sin that I should avoid?

P.ROMISE TO KEEP

Does God communicate a promise for me to claim?

E.XAMPLE TO FOLLOW

Do I find role models in this passage? What character traits and which actions are commendable? Which are not?

C.OMMAND TO OBEY

Are there any specific commands given for me to follow. What does God want me to apply to my life today and this week so that I develop Godly character and habits?

K. – KNOWLEDGE ABOUT GOD

What does this passage tell me about God or about Jesus Christ or the Holy Spirit? What is God like? What are His attributes? What does He do? What does He like and dislike? What is His attitude?

NOTE - you can't always answer all 5 parts.

STUDY

S. in to confess + avoid

_____
_____
_____
_____
_____
_____

P. romise to keep

_____
_____
_____
_____
_____
_____
_____
_____

E. xample to follow

_____
_____
_____
_____
_____
_____
_____
_____

STUDY

C. ommand to obey

_____
_____
_____
_____
_____
_____
_____
_____
_____
_____
_____

K. nowledge about God

_____
_____
_____
_____
_____
_____
_____
_____
_____
_____
_____
_____
_____
_____
_____
_____
_____
_____

TUNE IN

Relax, let go, be quiet before the Lord and listen.

This is a time of focus. Focus on the scripture and set your mind on the Father, Son, and Holy Spirit. Take as much time as you need. Don't rush this part! After some time has passed, use the space below to write anything God revealed or spoke to you.

_____
_____
_____
_____
_____
_____
_____
_____
_____
_____
_____
_____
_____
_____
_____
_____
_____
_____
_____
_____
_____
_____
_____
_____
_____
_____

LIVE

How can you apply this Word to your life?

Why does what I learned today matter? How do I implement it in my life today? How should my perspective change based on what I have learned? Look for applications that affect your relationship to God, with others, and your view of self. Use the space below to explore these questions.

ENCOURAGE

How I can share what I have learned to help someone else?

When do I plan to share this? Who do I plan to sharing this with? How do I plan to share this? In-person? Text message? Phone call? Social Media? Use the space below to develop a plan of action.

_____
_____
_____
_____
_____
_____
_____
_____
_____
_____
_____
_____
_____
_____
_____
_____
_____
_____
_____
_____
_____
_____
_____
_____
_____

Additional Notes:

Study H.U.S.T.L.E. Repeat

How to Study the Bible
The H.U.S.T.E. Way

H — **HUMBLE**
Humble yourself and pray.

U — **UNDERSTAND**
Look up different translations, definitions and cross references.

S — **STUDY**
What is the text saying to me?

T — **TUNE IN**
Relax, let go, be quiet before the Lord and listen.

L — **LIVE**
How can you apply this Word to your life?

E — **ENCOURAGE**
How I can share what I have learned to help someone else?

The H.U.S.T.L.E. Bible Study Method

Date:

HUMBLE
yourself and pray.

James 1:5, KJV:
"If any of you lack wisdom, let him ask of God, that giveth to all men liberally, and upbraideth not; and it shall be given him."

Lord, thank You for this time You've given me to open Your Word and discover who You are. Thank You that You don't leave us in the dark about who You are and what You are doing in the world, but that You have revealed Yourself and Your Will through the Bible, Your sacred Words to us.

Lord, I need wisdom as I read Your Word. You promise us in James 1:5 that we only have to ask for wisdom to receive it. Lord, please give me Your wisdom now as I approach Your Word. Help me discern the truth of this text. Help me not rely on my own understanding. Thank you God for the clarity, encouragement and hope Your Word brings.

In Jesus' Name I pray, Amen.

Use the space below to pray specifically about what you would like God to reveal through your Bible Study.

Dear Heavenly Father:

_____
_____
_____
_____
_____
_____
_____
_____
_____
_____
_____
_____
_____
_____
_____
_____
_____
_____
_____
_____
_____
_____
_____
_____
_____
_____
_____
_____

In Jesus Name I pray, Amen

UNDERSTAND
Look up different translations, definitions and cross references.

Scripture: _____

Use the space below to write out the scripture in your favorite translation, then choose another translation to write the scripture out.

Favorite Translation:

_____
_____
_____
_____
_____
_____
_____
_____
_____
_____

Another Translation:

_____
_____
_____
_____
_____
_____
_____
_____
_____
_____

Note any words that are different between the two translations. Use a Bible Dictionary to look up the words. Also read the cross-reference scriptures to dive deeper into the scripture and gain a better understanding.

UNDERSTAND

Words that stand out/are different per translation:

_____
_____
_____
_____
_____
_____
_____

Definitions:

_____
_____
_____
_____
_____
_____
_____
_____

Cross-Reference Scriptures:

_____
_____
_____
_____
_____
_____
_____
_____

STUDY
What is the text saying to me?

Use the S.P.E.C.K. Method to explore the text.

S.IN TO CONFESS + AVOID

In the passage, does God say something about sin? Is there a sin to confess? Is there a sin that I should avoid?

P.ROMISE TO KEEP

Does God communicate a promise for me to claim?

E.XAMPLE TO FOLLOW

Do I find role models in this passage? What character traits and which actions are commendable? Which are not?

C.OMMAND TO OBEY

Are there any specific commands given for me to follow. What does God want me to apply to my life today and this week so that I develop Godly character and habits?

K. – KNOWLEDGE ABOUT GOD

What does this passage tell me about God or about Jesus Christ or the Holy Spirit? What is God like? What are His attributes? What does He do? What does He like and dislike? What is His attitude?

NOTE - you can't always answer all 5 parts.

STUDY

S. in to confess + avoid

_____
_____
_____
_____
_____
_____
_____

P. romise to keep

_____
_____
_____
_____
_____
_____
_____
_____
_____

E. xample to follow

_____
_____
_____
_____
_____
_____
_____
_____
_____

STUDY

C. ommand to obey

_____
_____
_____
_____
_____
_____
_____
_____
_____
_____

K. nowledge about God

_____
_____
_____
_____
_____
_____
_____
_____
_____
_____
_____
_____
_____
_____
_____
_____

TUNE IN

Relax, let go, be quiet before the Lord and listen.

This is a time of focus. Focus on the scripture and set your mind on the Father, Son, and Holy Spirit. Take as much time as you need. Don't rush this part! After some time has passed, use the space below to write anything God revealed or spoke to you.

_____
_____
_____
_____
_____
_____
_____
_____
_____
_____
_____
_____
_____
_____
_____
_____
_____
_____
_____
_____
_____
_____
_____
_____
_____
_____
_____
_____
_____

LIVE

How can you apply this Word to your life?

Why does what I learned today matter? How do I implement it in my life today? How should my perspective change based on what I have learned? Look for applications that affect your relationship to God, with others, and your view of self. Use the space below to explore these questions.

_____
_____
_____
_____
_____
_____
_____
_____
_____
_____
_____
_____
_____
_____
_____
_____
_____
_____
_____
_____
_____
_____
_____
_____
_____
_____
_____

ENCOURAGE

How I can share what I have learned to help someone else?

When do I plan to share this? Who do I plan to sharing this with? How do I plan to share this? In-person? Text message? Phone call? Social Media? Use the space below to develop a plan of action.

_____
_____
_____
_____
_____
_____
_____
_____
_____
_____
_____
_____
_____
_____
_____
_____
_____
_____
_____
_____
_____
_____
_____
_____

Additional Notes:

How to Study the Bible
The **H.U.S.T.L.E.** Way

H — **HUMBLE**
Humble yourself and pray.

U — **UNDERSTAND**
Look up different translations, definitions and cross references.

S — **STUDY**
What is the text saying to me?

T — **TUNE IN**
Relax, let go, be quiet before the Lord and listen.

L — **LIVE**
How can you apply this Word to your life?

E — **ENCOURAGE**
How I can share what I have learned to help someone else?

Date:

HUMBLE
yourself and pray.

James 1:5, KJV:
"If any of you lack wisdom, let him ask of God, that giveth to all men liberally, and upbraideth not; and it shall be given him."

Lord, thank You for this time You've given me to open Your Word and discover who You are. Thank You that You don't leave us in the dark about who You are and what You are doing in the world, but that You have revealed Yourself and Your Will through the Bible, Your sacred Words to us.

Lord, I need wisdom as I read Your Word. You promise us in James 1:5 that we only have to ask for wisdom to receive it. Lord, please give me Your wisdom now as I approach Your Word. Help me discern the truth of this text. Help me not rely on my own understanding. Thank you God for the clarity, encouragement and hope Your Word brings.

In Jesus' Name I pray, Amen.

Use the space below to pray specifically about what you would like God to reveal through your Bible Study.

Dear Heavenly Father:

In Jesus Name I pray, Amen

UNDERSTAND

Look up different translations, definitions and cross references.

Scripture: _____

Use the space below to write out the scripture in your favorite translation, then choose another translation to write the scripture out.

Favorite Translation:

_____
_____
_____
_____
_____
_____
_____
_____
_____

Another Translation:

_____
_____
_____
_____
_____
_____
_____
_____
_____

Note any words that are different between the two translations. Use a Bible Dictionary to look up the words. Also read the cross-reference scriptures to dive deeper into the scripture and gain a better understanding.

UNDERSTAND

Words that stand out/are different per translation:
_____
_____
_____
_____
_____
_____
_____

Definitions:
_____
_____
_____
_____
_____
_____
_____
_____

Cross-Reference Scriptures:
_____
_____
_____
_____
_____
_____
_____
_____

STUDY

What is the text saying to me?

Use the S.P.E.C.K. Method to explore the text.

S.IN TO CONFESS + AVOID

In the passage, does God say something about sin? Is there a sin to confess? Is there a sin that I should avoid?

P.ROMISE TO KEEP

Does God communicate a promise for me to claim?

E.XAMPLE TO FOLLOW

Do I find role models in this passage? What character traits and which actions are commendable? Which are not?

C.OMMAND TO OBEY

Are there any specific commands given for me to follow. What does God want me to apply to my life today and this week so that I develop Godly character and habits?

K. – KNOWLEDGE ABOUT GOD

What does this passage tell me about God or about Jesus Christ or the Holy Spirit? What is God like? What are His attributes? What does He do? What does He like and dislike? What is His attitude?

NOTE - you can't always answer all 5 parts.

STUDY

S. in to confess + avoid

_____
_____
_____
_____
_____
_____
_____

P. romise to keep

_____
_____
_____
_____
_____
_____
_____

E. xample to follow

_____
_____
_____
_____
_____
_____
_____

STUDY

C. ommand to obey

_____
_____
_____
_____
_____
_____
_____
_____
_____
_____

K. nowledge about God

_____
_____
_____
_____
_____
_____
_____
_____
_____
_____
_____
_____
_____
_____
_____

TUNE IN

Relax, let go, be quiet before the Lord and listen.

This is a time of focus. Focus on the scripture and set your mind on the Father, Son, and Holy Spirit. Take as much time as you need. Don't rush this part! After some time has passed, use the space below to write anything God revealed or spoke to you.

_____
_____
_____
_____
_____
_____
_____
_____
_____
_____
_____
_____
_____
_____
_____
_____
_____
_____
_____
_____
_____
_____
_____
_____
_____
_____
_____

LIVE

How can you apply this Word to your life?

Why does what I learned today matter? How do I implement it in my life today? How should my perspective change based on what I have learned? Look for applications that affect your relationship to God, with others, and your view of self. Use the space below to explore these questions.

ENCOURAGE
How I can share what I have learned to help someone else?

When do I plan to share this? Who do I plan to sharing this with? How do I plan to share this? In-person? Text message? Phone call? Social Media? Use the space below to develop a plan of action.

_____
_____
_____
_____
_____
_____
_____
_____
_____
_____
_____
_____
_____
_____
_____
_____
_____
_____
_____
_____
_____
_____
_____
_____

Additional Notes:

Study H.U.S.T.L.E. Repeat

How to Study the Bible
The H.U.S.T.E. Way

H — **HUMBLE**
Humble yourself and pray.

U — **UNDERSTAND**
Look up different translations, definitions and cross references.

S — **STUDY**
What is the text saying to me?

T — **TUNE IN**
Relax, let go, be quiet before the Lord and listen.

L — **LIVE**
How can you apply this Word to your life?

E — **ENCOURAGE**
How I can share what I have learned to help someone else?

The H.U.S.T.L.E. Bible Study Method

Date:

HUMBLE
yourself and pray.

James 1:5, KJV:
"If any of you lack wisdom, let him ask of God, that giveth to all men liberally, and upbraideth not; and it shall be given him."

Lord, thank You for this time You've given me to open Your Word and discover who You are. Thank You that You don't leave us in the dark about who You are and what You are doing in the world, but that You have revealed Yourself and Your Will through the Bible, Your sacred Words to us.

Lord, I need wisdom as I read Your Word. You promise us in James 1:5 that we only have to ask for wisdom to receive it. Lord, please give me Your wisdom now as I approach Your Word. Help me discern the truth of this text. Help me not rely on my own understanding. Thank you God for the clarity, encouragement and hope Your Word brings.

In Jesus' Name I pray, Amen.

Use the space below to pray specifically about what you would like God to reveal through your Bible Study.

Dear Heavenly Father:

_____
_____
_____
_____
_____
_____
_____
_____
_____
_____
_____
_____
_____
_____
_____
_____
_____
_____
_____
_____
_____
_____
_____
_____
_____
_____
_____
_____
_____

In Jesus Name I pray, Amen

UNDERSTAND
Look up different translations, definitions and cross references.

Scripture: _____

Use the space below to write out the scripture in your favorite translation, then choose another translation to write the scripture out.

Favorite Translation:

_____
_____
_____
_____
_____
_____
_____
_____
_____
_____

Another Translation:

_____
_____
_____
_____
_____
_____
_____
_____
_____
_____

Note any words that are different between the two translations. Use a Bible Dictionary to look up the words. Also read the cross-reference scriptures to dive deeper into the scripture and gain a better understanding.

UNDERSTAND

Words that stand out/are different per translation:

_____
_____
_____
_____
_____
_____
_____

Definitions:

_____
_____
_____
_____
_____
_____
_____
_____

Cross-Reference Scriptures:

_____
_____
_____
_____
_____
_____
_____
_____

STUDY

What is the text saying to me?

Use the S.P.E.C.K. Method to explore the text.

S.IN TO CONFESS + AVOID

In the passage, does God say something about sin? Is there a sin to confess? Is there a sin that I should avoid?

P.ROMISE TO KEEP

Does God communicate a promise for me to claim?

E.XAMPLE TO FOLLOW

Do I find role models in this passage? What character traits and which actions are commendable? Which are not?

C.OMMAND TO OBEY

Are there any specific commands given for me to follow. What does God want me to apply to my life today and this week so that I develop Godly character and habits?

K. – KNOWLEDGE ABOUT GOD

What does this passage tell me about God or about Jesus Christ or the Holy Spirit? What is God like? What are His attributes? What does He do? What does He like and dislike? What is His attitude?

NOTE - you can't always answer all 5 parts.

STUDY

S. in to confess + avoid

_____
_____
_____
_____
_____
_____
_____

P. romise to keep

_____
_____
_____
_____
_____
_____
_____
_____

E. xample to follow

_____
_____
_____
_____
_____
_____
_____
_____

STUDY

C. ommand to obey

_____
_____
_____
_____
_____
_____
_____
_____
_____

K. nowledge about God

_____
_____
_____
_____
_____
_____
_____
_____
_____
_____
_____
_____
_____

TUNE IN

Relax, let go, be quiet before the Lord and listen.

This is a time of focus. Focus on the scripture and set your mind on the Father, Son, and Holy Spirit. Take as much time as you need. Don't rush this part! After some time has passed, use the space below to write anything God revealed or spoke to you.

_____
_____
_____
_____
_____
_____
_____
_____
_____
_____
_____
_____
_____
_____
_____
_____
_____
_____
_____
_____
_____
_____
_____
_____
_____
_____
_____
_____
_____
_____

LIVE

How can you apply this Word to your life?

Why does what I learned today matter? How do I implement it in my life today? How should my perspective change based on what I have learned? Look for applications that affect your relationship to God, with others, and your view of self. Use the space below to explore these questions.

_____
_____
_____
_____
_____
_____
_____
_____
_____
_____
_____
_____
_____
_____
_____
_____
_____
_____
_____
_____
_____
_____
_____
_____
_____
_____

ENCOURAGE

How I can share what I have learned to help someone else?

When do I plan to share this? Who do I plan to sharing this with? How do I plan to share this? In-person? Text message? Phone call? Social Media? Use the space below to develop a plan of action.

_____
_____
_____
_____
_____
_____
_____
_____
_____
_____
_____
_____
_____
_____
_____
_____
_____
_____
_____
_____
_____
_____
_____
_____
_____
_____

Additional Notes:

Study H.U.S.T.L.E. Repeat

How to Study the Bible
The H.U.S.T.L.E. Way

H — **HUMBLE**
Humble yourself and pray.

U — **UNDERSTAND**
Look up different translations, definitions and cross references.

S — **STUDY**
What is the text saying to me?

T — **TUNE IN**
Relax, let go, be quiet before the Lord and listen.

L — **LIVE**
How can you apply this Word to your life?

E — **ENCOURAGE**
How I can share what I have learned to help someone else?

The H.U.S.T.L.E. Bible Study Method

Date:

HUMBLE
yourself and pray.

James 1:5, KJV:
"If any of you lack wisdom, let him ask of God, that giveth to all men liberally, and upbraideth not; and it shall be given him."

Lord, thank You for this time You've given me to open Your Word and discover who You are. Thank You that You don't leave us in the dark about who You are and what You are doing in the world, but that You have revealed Yourself and Your Will through the Bible, Your sacred Words to us.

Lord, I need wisdom as I read Your Word. You promise us in James 1:5 that we only have to ask for wisdom to receive it. Lord, please give me Your wisdom now as I approach Your Word. Help me discern the truth of this text. Help me not rely on my own understanding. Thank you God for the clarity, encouragement and hope Your Word brings.

In Jesus' Name I pray, Amen.

Use the space below to pray specifically about what you would like God to reveal through your Bible Study.

Dear Heavenly Father:

_____
_____
_____
_____
_____
_____
_____
_____
_____
_____
_____
_____
_____
_____
_____
_____
_____
_____
_____
_____
_____
_____
_____
_____
_____
_____
_____
_____

In Jesus Name I pray, Amen

UNDERSTAND
Look up different translations, definitions and cross references.

Scripture: _____

Use the space below to write out the scripture in your favorite translation, then choose another translation to write the scripture out.

Favorite Translation:

_____
_____
_____
_____
_____
_____
_____
_____
_____
_____

Another Translation:

_____
_____
_____
_____
_____
_____
_____
_____
_____
_____

Note any words that are different between the two translations. Use a Bible Dictionary to look up the words. Also read the cross-reference scriptures to dive deeper into the scripture and gain a better understanding.

UNDERSTAND

Words that stand out/are different per translation:

_____
_____
_____
_____
_____
_____
_____
_____

Definitions:

_____
_____
_____
_____
_____
_____
_____
_____
_____

Cross-Reference Scriptures:

_____
_____
_____
_____
_____
_____
_____
_____
_____

STUDY

What is the text saying to me?

Use the S.P.E.C.K. Method to explore the text.

S.IN TO CONFESS + AVOID

In the passage, does God say something about sin? Is there a sin to confess? Is there a sin that I should avoid?

P.ROMISE TO KEEP

Does God communicate a promise for me to claim?

E.XAMPLE TO FOLLOW

Do I find role models in this passage? What character traits and which actions are commendable? Which are not?

C.OMMAND TO OBEY

Are there any specific commands given for me to follow. What does God want me to apply to my life today and this week so that I develop Godly character and habits?

K. – KNOWLEDGE ABOUT GOD

What does this passage tell me about God or about Jesus Christ or the Holy Spirit? What is God like? What are His attributes? What does He do? What does He like and dislike? What is His attitude?

NOTE - you can't always answer all 5 parts.

STUDY

S. in to confess + avoid

_____
_____
_____
_____
_____
_____

P. romise to keep

_____
_____
_____
_____
_____
_____

E. xample to follow

_____
_____
_____
_____
_____
_____
_____

STUDY

C. ommand to obey

_____
_____
_____
_____
_____
_____
_____
_____
_____

K. nowledge about God

_____
_____
_____
_____
_____
_____
_____
_____
_____
_____
_____

TUNE IN

Relax, let go, be quiet before the Lord and listen.

This is a time of focus. Focus on the scripture and set your mind on the Father, Son, and Holy Spirit. Take as much time as you need. Don't rush this part! After some time has passed, use the space below to write anything God revealed or spoke to you.

_____
_____
_____
_____
_____
_____
_____
_____
_____
_____
_____
_____
_____
_____
_____
_____
_____
_____
_____
_____
_____
_____
_____
_____
_____

LIVE

How can you apply this Word to your life?

Why does what I learned today matter? How do I implement it in my life today? How should my perspective change based on what I have learned? Look for applications that affect your relationship to God, with others, and your view of self. Use the space below to explore these questions.

ENCOURAGE

How I can share what I have learned to help someone else?

When do I plan to share this? Who do I plan to sharing this with? How do I plan to share this? In-person? Text message? Phone call? Social Media? Use the space below to develop a plan of action.

_____
_____
_____
_____
_____
_____
_____
_____
_____
_____
_____
_____
_____
_____
_____
_____
_____
_____
_____
_____
_____
_____
_____
_____
_____
_____

Additional Notes:

_____
_____
_____
_____
_____
_____
_____
_____
_____
_____
_____
_____
_____
_____
_____
_____
_____
_____
_____
_____
_____
_____
_____
_____
_____
_____
_____
_____

Study H.U.S.T.L.E. Repeat

How to Study the Bible
The **H.U.S.T.L.E.** Way

H — **HUMBLE**
Humble yourself and pray.

U — **UNDERSTAND**
Look up different translations, definitions and cross references.

S — **STUDY**
What is the text saying to me?

T — **TUNE IN**
Relax, let go, be quiet before the Lord and listen.

L — **LIVE**
How can you apply this Word to your life?

E — **ENCOURAGE**
How I can share what I have learned to help someone else?

Date:

HUMBLE
yourself and pray.

James 1:5, KJV:
"If any of you lack wisdom, let him ask of God, that giveth to all men liberally, and upbraideth not; and it shall be given him."

Lord, thank You for this time You've given me to open Your Word and discover who You are. Thank You that You don't leave us in the dark about who You are and what You are doing in the world, but that You have revealed Yourself and Your Will through the Bible, Your sacred Words to us.

Lord, I need wisdom as I read Your Word. You promise us in James 1:5 that we only have to ask for wisdom to receive it. Lord, please give me Your wisdom now as I approach Your Word. Help me discern the truth of this text. Help me not rely on my own understanding. Thank you God for the clarity, encouragement and hope Your Word brings.

In Jesus' Name I pray, Amen.

Use the space below to pray specifically about what you would like God to reveal through your Bible Study.

Dear Heavenly Father:

In Jesus Name I pray, Amen

UNDERSTAND

Look up different translations, definitions and cross references.

Scripture: _____

Use the space below to write out the scripture in your favorite translation, then choose another translation to write the scripture out.

Favorite Translation:

_____
_____
_____
_____
_____
_____
_____
_____

Another Translation:

_____
_____
_____
_____
_____
_____
_____
_____

Note any words that are different between the two translations. Use a Bible Dictionary to look up the words. Also read the cross-reference scriptures to dive deeper into the scripture and gain a better understanding.

UNDERSTAND

Words that stand out/are different per translation:

_____
_____
_____
_____
_____
_____
_____

Definitions:

_____
_____
_____
_____
_____
_____
_____

Cross-Reference Scriptures:

_____
_____
_____
_____
_____
_____
_____

Study H.U.S.T.L.E. Repeat

STUDY

What is the text saying to me?

Use the S.P.E.C.K. Method to explore the text.

S.IN TO CONFESS + AVOID

In the passage, does God say something about sin? Is there a sin to confess? Is there a sin that I should avoid?

P.ROMISE TO KEEP

Does God communicate a promise for me to claim?

E.XAMPLE TO FOLLOW

Do I find role models in this passage? What character traits and which actions are commendable? Which are not?

C.OMMAND TO OBEY

Are there any specific commands given for me to follow. What does God want me to apply to my life today and this week so that I develop Godly character and habits?

K. – KNOWLEDGE ABOUT GOD

What does this passage tell me about God or about Jesus Christ or the Holy Spirit? What is God like? What are His attributes? What does He do? What does He like and dislike? What is His attitude?

NOTE - you can't always answer all 5 parts.

STUDY

S. in to confess + avoid

_____
_____
_____
_____
_____
_____

P. romise to keep

_____
_____
_____
_____
_____
_____

E. xample to follow

_____
_____
_____
_____
_____
_____

STUDY

C. ommand to obey

_____
_____
_____
_____
_____
_____
_____
_____
_____
_____

K. nowledge about God

_____
_____
_____
_____
_____
_____
_____
_____
_____
_____
_____
_____
_____
_____

TUNE IN

Relax, let go, be quiet before the Lord and listen.

This is a time of focus. Focus on the scripture and set your mind on the Father, Son, and Holy Spirit. Take as much time as you need. Don't rush this part! After some time has passed, use the space below to write anything God revealed or spoke to you.

_____
_____
_____
_____
_____
_____
_____
_____
_____
_____
_____
_____
_____
_____
_____
_____
_____
_____
_____
_____
_____
_____
_____
_____

LIVE

How can you apply this Word to your life?

Why does what I learned today matter? How do I implement it in my life today? How should my perspective change based on what I have learned? Look for applications that affect your relationship to God, with others, and your view of self. Use the space below to explore these questions.

ENCOURAGE

How I can share what I have learned to help someone else?

When do I plan to share this? Who do I plan to sharing this with? How do I plan to share this? In-person? Text message? Phone call? Social Media? Use the space below to develop a plan of action.

_____
_____
_____
_____
_____
_____
_____
_____
_____
_____
_____
_____
_____
_____
_____
_____
_____
_____
_____
_____
_____
_____
_____
_____
_____

Additional Notes:

How to Study the Bible
The **H.U.S.T.L.E.** Way

H — **HUMBLE**
Humble yourself and pray.

U — **UNDERSTAND**
Look up different translations, definitions and cross references.

S — **STUDY**
What is the text saying to me?

T — **TUNE IN**
Relax, let go, be quiet before the Lord and listen.

L — **LIVE**
How can you apply this Word to your life?

E — **ENCOURAGE**
How I can share what I have learned to help someone else?

The H.U.S.T.L.E. Bible Study Method

Date:

HUMBLE
yourself and pray.

James 1:5, KJV:
"If any of you lack wisdom, let him ask of God, that giveth to all men liberally, and upbraideth not; and it shall be given him."

Lord, thank You for this time You've given me to open Your Word and discover who You are. Thank You that You don't leave us in the dark about who You are and what You are doing in the world, but that You have revealed Yourself and Your Will through the Bible, Your sacred Words to us.

Lord, I need wisdom as I read Your Word. You promise us in James 1:5 that we only have to ask for wisdom to receive it. Lord, please give me Your wisdom now as I approach Your Word. Help me discern the truth of this text. Help me not rely on my own understanding. Thank you God for the clarity, encouragement and hope Your Word brings.

In Jesus' Name I pray, Amen.

Use the space below to pray specifically about what you would like God to reveal through your Bible Study.

Dear Heavenly Father:

_____
_____
_____
_____
_____
_____
_____
_____
_____
_____
_____
_____
_____
_____
_____
_____
_____
_____
_____
_____
_____
_____
_____
_____
_____
_____

In Jesus Name I pray, Amen

UNDERSTAND
Look up different translations, definitions and cross references.

Scripture: _____

Use the space below to write out the scripture in your favorite translation, then choose another translation to write the scripture out.

Favorite Translation:

_____
_____
_____
_____
_____
_____
_____
_____
_____
_____

Another Translation:

_____
_____
_____
_____
_____
_____
_____
_____
_____
_____

Note any words that are different between the two translations. Use a Bible Dictionary to look up the words. Also read the cross-reference scriptures to dive deeper into the scripture and gain a better understanding.

UNDERSTAND

Words that stand out/are different per translation:
_____
_____
_____
_____
_____
_____
_____

Definitions:
_____
_____
_____
_____
_____
_____
_____
_____

Cross-Reference Scriptures:
_____
_____
_____
_____
_____
_____
_____
_____

STUDY

What is the text saying to me?

Use the S.P.E.C.K. Method to explore the text.

S.IN TO CONFESS + AVOID

In the passage, does God say something about sin? Is there a sin to confess? Is there a sin that I should avoid?

P.ROMISE TO KEEP

Does God communicate a promise for me to claim?

E.XAMPLE TO FOLLOW

Do I find role models in this passage? What character traits and which actions are commendable? Which are not?

C.OMMAND TO OBEY

Are there any specific commands given for me to follow. What does God want me to apply to my life today and this week so that I develop Godly character and habits?

K. – KNOWLEDGE ABOUT GOD

What does this passage tell me about God or about Jesus Christ or the Holy Spirit? What is God like? What are His attributes? What does He do? What does He like and dislike? What is His attitude?

NOTE - you can't always answer all 5 parts.

STUDY

S. in to confess + avoid

_____
_____
_____
_____
_____

P. romise to keep

_____
_____
_____
_____
_____
_____
_____

E. xample to follow

_____
_____
_____
_____
_____
_____

STUDY

C. ommand to obey

_____
_____
_____
_____
_____
_____
_____
_____
_____
_____

K. nowledge about God

_____
_____
_____
_____
_____
_____
_____
_____
_____
_____
_____
_____
_____
_____
_____

TUNE IN

Relax, let go, be quiet before the Lord and listen.

This is a time of focus. Focus on the scripture and set your mind on the Father, Son, and Holy Spirit. Take as much time as you need. Don't rush this part! After some time has passed, use the space below to write anything God revealed or spoke to you.

_____
_____
_____
_____
_____
_____
_____
_____
_____
_____
_____
_____
_____
_____
_____
_____
_____
_____
_____
_____
_____
_____
_____
_____

LIVE

How can you apply this Word to your life?

Why does what I learned today matter? How do I implement it in my life today? How should my perspective change based on what I have learned? Look for applications that affect your relationship to God, with others, and your view of self. Use the space below to explore these questions.

ENCOURAGE

How I can share what I have learned to help someone else?

When do I plan to share this? Who do I plan to sharing this with? How do I plan to share this? In-person? Text message? Phone call? Social Media? Use the space below to develop a plan of action.

_____
_____
_____
_____
_____
_____
_____
_____
_____
_____
_____
_____
_____
_____
_____
_____
_____
_____
_____
_____
_____
_____
_____
_____
_____
_____
_____
_____

Additional Notes:

Study H.U.S.T.L.E. Repeat

How to Study the Bible
The H.U.S.T.L.E. Way

H — HUMBLE
Humble yourself and pray.

U — UNDERSTAND
Look up different translations, definitions and cross references.

S — STUDY
What is the text saying to me?

T — TUNE IN
Relax, let go, be quiet before the Lord and listen.

L — LIVE
How can you apply this Word to your life?

E — ENCOURAGE
How I can share what I have learned to help someone else?

The H.U.S.T.L.E. Bible Study Method

Date:

HUMBLE
yourself and pray.

James 1:5, KJV:
"If any of you lack wisdom, let him ask of God, that giveth to all men liberally, and upbraideth not; and it shall be given him."

Lord, thank You for this time You've given me to open Your Word and discover who You are. Thank You that You don't leave us in the dark about who You are and what You are doing in the world, but that You have revealed Yourself and Your Will through the Bible, Your sacred Words to us.

Lord, I need wisdom as I read Your Word. You promise us in James 1:5 that we only have to ask for wisdom to receive it. Lord, please give me Your wisdom now as I approach Your Word. Help me discern the truth of this text. Help me not rely on my own understanding. Thank you God for the clarity, encouragement and hope Your Word brings.

In Jesus' Name I pray, Amen.

Use the space below to pray specifically about what you would like God to reveal through your Bible Study.

Dear Heavenly Father:

_____
_____
_____
_____
_____
_____
_____
_____
_____
_____
_____
_____
_____
_____
_____
_____
_____
_____
_____
_____
_____
_____
_____
_____
_____
_____

In Jesus Name I pray, Amen

UNDERSTAND
Look up different translations, definitions and cross references.

Scripture: _____

Use the space below to write out the scripture in your favorite translation, then choose another translation to write the scripture out.

Favorite Translation:
_____
_____
_____
_____
_____
_____
_____
_____

Another Translation:
_____
_____
_____
_____
_____
_____
_____
_____

Note any words that are different between the two translations. Use a Bible Dictionary to look up the words. Also read the cross-reference scriptures to dive deeper into the scripture and gain a better understanding.

UNDERSTAND

Words that stand out/are different per translation:
_____
_____
_____
_____
_____
_____
_____

Definitions:
_____
_____
_____
_____
_____
_____
_____
_____

Cross-Reference Scriptures:
_____
_____
_____
_____
_____
_____
_____
_____

STUDY

What is the text saying to me?

Use the S.P.E.C.K. Method to explore the text.

S.IN TO CONFESS + AVOID

In the passage, does God say something about sin? Is there a sin to confess? Is there a sin that I should avoid?

P.ROMISE TO KEEP

Does God communicate a promise for me to claim?

E.XAMPLE TO FOLLOW

Do I find role models in this passage? What character traits and which actions are commendable? Which are not?

C.OMMAND TO OBEY

Are there any specific commands given for me to follow. What does God want me to apply to my life today and this week so that I develop Godly character and habits?

K. – KNOWLEDGE ABOUT GOD

What does this passage tell me about God or about Jesus Christ or the Holy Spirit? What is God like? What are His attributes? What does He do? What does He like and dislike? What is His attitude?

NOTE - you can't always answer all 5 parts.

STUDY

S. in to confess + avoid

_____
_____
_____
_____
_____
_____

P. romise to keep

_____
_____
_____
_____
_____
_____

E. xample to follow

_____
_____
_____
_____
_____
_____

STUDY

C. ommand to obey

_____
_____
_____
_____
_____
_____
_____
_____
_____

K. nowledge about God

_____
_____
_____
_____
_____
_____
_____
_____
_____
_____
_____
_____
_____
_____
_____
_____

TUNE IN

Relax, let go, be quiet before the Lord and listen.

This is a time of focus. Focus on the scripture and set your mind on the Father, Son, and Holy Spirit. Take as much time as you need. Don't rush this part! After some time has passed, use the space below to write anything God revealed or spoke to you.

_____
_____
_____
_____
_____
_____
_____
_____
_____
_____
_____
_____
_____
_____
_____
_____
_____
_____
_____
_____
_____
_____
_____
_____

LIVE

How can you apply this Word to your life?

Why does what I learned today matter? How do I implement it in my life today? How should my perspective change based on what I have learned? Look for applications that affect your relationship to God, with others, and your view of self. Use the space below to explore these questions.

ENCOURAGE

How I can share what I have learned to help someone else?

When do I plan to share this? Who do I plan to sharing this with? How do I plan to share this? In-person? Text message? Phone call? Social Media? Use the space below to develop a plan of action.

_____
_____
_____
_____
_____
_____
_____
_____
_____
_____
_____
_____
_____
_____
_____
_____
_____
_____
_____
_____
_____
_____
_____
_____
_____
_____
_____
_____
_____

Additional Notes:

Study H.U.S.T.L.E. Repeat

How to Study the Bible
The H.U.S.T.L.E. Way

H — HUMBLE
Humble yourself and pray.

U — UNDERSTAND
Look up different translations, definitions and cross references.

S — STUDY
What is the text saying to me?

T — TUNE IN
Relax, let go, be quiet before the Lord and listen.

L — LIVE
How can you apply this Word to your life?

E — ENCOURAGE
How I can share what I have learned to help someone else?

The H.U.S.T.L.E. Bible Study Method

Date:

HUMBLE
yourself and pray.

James 1:5, KJV:
"If any of you lack wisdom, let him ask of God, that giveth to all men liberally, and upbraideth not; and it shall be given him."

Lord, thank You for this time You've given me to open Your Word and discover who You are. Thank You that You don't leave us in the dark about who You are and what You are doing in the world, but that You have revealed Yourself and Your Will through the Bible, Your sacred Words to us.

Lord, I need wisdom as I read Your Word. You promise us in James 1:5 that we only have to ask for wisdom to receive it. Lord, please give me Your wisdom now as I approach Your Word. Help me discern the truth of this text. Help me not rely on my own understanding. Thank you God for the clarity, encouragement and hope Your Word brings.

In Jesus' Name I pray, Amen.

Use the space below to pray specifically about what you would like God to reveal through your Bible Study.

Dear Heavenly Father:

_____
_____
_____
_____
_____
_____
_____
_____
_____
_____
_____
_____
_____
_____
_____
_____
_____
_____
_____
_____
_____
_____
_____
_____
_____
_____
_____

In Jesus Name I pray, Amen

UNDERSTAND

Look up different translations, definitions and cross references.

Scripture: _____

Use the space below to write out the scripture in your favorite translation, then choose another translation to write the scripture out.

Favorite Translation:
_____
_____
_____
_____
_____
_____
_____
_____

Another Translation:
_____
_____
_____
_____
_____
_____
_____
_____

Note any words that are different between the two translations. Use a Bible Dictionary to look up the words. Also read the cross-reference scriptures to dive deeper into the scripture and gain a better understanding.

UNDERSTAND

Words that stand out/are different per translation:
_____
_____
_____
_____
_____
_____
_____
_____

Definitions:
_____
_____
_____
_____
_____
_____
_____
_____

Cross-Reference Scriptures:
_____
_____
_____
_____
_____
_____
_____
_____

STUDY

What is the text saying to me?

Use the S.P.E.C.K. Method to explore the text.

S.IN TO CONFESS + AVOID

In the passage, does God say something about sin? Is there a sin to confess? Is there a sin that I should avoid?

P.ROMISE TO KEEP

Does God communicate a promise for me to claim?

E.XAMPLE TO FOLLOW

Do I find role models in this passage? What character traits and which actions are commendable? Which are not?

C.OMMAND TO OBEY

Are there any specific commands given for me to follow. What does God want me to apply to my life today and this week so that I develop Godly character and habits?

K. – KNOWLEDGE ABOUT GOD

What does this passage tell me about God or about Jesus Christ or the Holy Spirit? What is God like? What are His attributes? What does He do? What does He like and dislike? What is His attitude?

NOTE - you can't always answer all 5 parts.

STUDY

S. in to confess + avoid

_____
_____
_____
_____
_____
_____

P. romise to keep

_____
_____
_____
_____
_____
_____
_____

E. xample to follow

_____
_____
_____
_____
_____
_____
_____

STUDY

C. ommand to obey

_____
_____
_____
_____
_____
_____
_____
_____
_____
_____
_____

K. nowledge about God

_____
_____
_____
_____
_____
_____
_____
_____
_____
_____
_____
_____
_____
_____
_____
_____

TUNE IN

Relax, let go, be quiet before the Lord and listen.

This is a time of focus. Focus on the scripture and set your mind on the Father, Son, and Holy Spirit. Take as much time as you need. Don't rush this part! After some time has passed, use the space below to write anything God revealed or spoke to you.

_____
_____
_____
_____
_____
_____
_____
_____
_____
_____
_____
_____
_____
_____
_____
_____
_____
_____
_____
_____
_____
_____
_____
_____
_____

LIVE

How can you apply this Word to your life?

Why does what I learned today matter? How do I implement it in my life today? How should my perspective change based on what I have learned? Look for applications that affect your relationship to God, with others, and your view of self. Use the space below to explore these questions.

_____
_____
_____
_____
_____
_____
_____
_____
_____
_____
_____
_____
_____
_____
_____
_____
_____
_____
_____
_____
_____
_____
_____
_____
_____

ENCOURAGE

How I can share what I have learned to help someone else?

When do I plan to share this? Who do I plan to sharing this with? How do I plan to share this? In-person? Text message? Phone call? Social Media? Use the space below to develop a plan of action.

_____
_____
_____
_____
_____
_____
_____
_____
_____
_____
_____
_____
_____
_____
_____
_____
_____
_____
_____
_____
_____
_____
_____
_____
_____
_____

Additional Notes:

How to Study the Bible
The **H.U.S.T.L.E.** Way

H

HUMBLE
Humble yourself and pray.

U

UNDERSTAND
Look up different translations, definitions and cross references.

S

STUDY
What is the text saying to me?

T

TUNE IN
Relax, let go, be quiet before the Lord and listen.

L

LIVE
How can you apply this Word to your life?

E

ENCOURAGE
How I can share what I have learned to help someone else?

The H.U.S.T.L.E. Bible Study Method

Date:

HUMBLE
yourself and pray.

James 1:5, KJV:
"If any of you lack wisdom, let him ask of God, that giveth to all men liberally, and upbraideth not; and it shall be given him."

Lord, thank You for this time You've given me to open Your Word and discover who You are. Thank You that You don't leave us in the dark about who You are and what You are doing in the world, but that You have revealed Yourself and Your Will through the Bible, Your sacred Words to us.

Lord, I need wisdom as I read Your Word. You promise us in James 1:5 that we only have to ask for wisdom to receive it. Lord, please give me Your wisdom now as I approach Your Word. Help me discern the truth of this text. Help me not rely on my own understanding. Thank you God for the clarity, encouragement and hope Your Word brings.

In Jesus' Name I pray, Amen.

Use the space below to pray specifically about what you would like God to reveal through your Bible Study.

Dear Heavenly Father:

_____
_____
_____
_____
_____
_____
_____
_____
_____
_____
_____
_____
_____
_____
_____
_____
_____
_____
_____
_____
_____
_____
_____
_____
_____
_____
_____

In Jesus Name I pray, Amen

UNDERSTAND
Look up different translations, definitions and cross references.

Scripture: _____

Use the space below to write out the scripture in your favorite translation, then choose another translation to write the scripture out.

Favorite Translation:

_____
_____
_____
_____
_____
_____
_____
_____
_____
_____

Another Translation:

_____
_____
_____
_____
_____
_____
_____
_____
_____
_____

Note any words that are different between the two translations. Use a Bible Dictionary to look up the words. Also read the cross-reference scriptures to dive deeper into the scripture and gain a better understanding.

UNDERSTAND

Words that stand out/are different per translation:

_____
_____
_____
_____
_____
_____
_____
_____

Definitions:

_____
_____
_____
_____
_____
_____
_____
_____
_____

Cross-Reference Scriptures:

_____
_____
_____
_____
_____
_____
_____
_____
_____

STUDY

What is the text saying to me?

Use the S.P.E.C.K. Method to explore the text.

S.IN TO CONFESS + AVOID

In the passage, does God say something about sin? Is there a sin to confess? Is there a sin that I should avoid?

P.ROMISE TO KEEP

Does God communicate a promise for me to claim?

E.XAMPLE TO FOLLOW

Do I find role models in this passage? What character traits and which actions are commendable? Which are not?

C.OMMAND TO OBEY

Are there any specific commands given for me to follow. What does God want me to apply to my life today and this week so that I develop Godly character and habits?

K. – KNOWLEDGE ABOUT GOD

What does this passage tell me about God or about Jesus Christ or the Holy Spirit? What is God like? What are His attributes? What does He do? What does He like and dislike? What is His attitude?

NOTE - you can't always answer all 5 parts.

STUDY

S. in to confess + avoid

_____
_____
_____
_____
_____
_____
_____

P. romise to keep

_____
_____
_____
_____
_____
_____
_____

E. xample to follow

_____
_____
_____
_____
_____
_____
_____

STUDY

C. ommand to obey

_____
_____
_____
_____
_____
_____
_____
_____
_____

K. nowledge about God

_____
_____
_____
_____
_____
_____
_____
_____
_____
_____
_____
_____
_____

TUNE IN

Relax, let go, be quiet before the Lord and listen.

This is a time of focus. Focus on the scripture and set your mind on the Father, Son, and Holy Spirit. Take as much time as you need. Don't rush this part! After some time has passed, use the space below to write anything God revealed or spoke to you.

_____
_____
_____
_____
_____
_____
_____
_____
_____
_____
_____
_____
_____
_____
_____
_____
_____
_____
_____
_____
_____
_____
_____
_____

LIVE

How can you apply this Word to your life?

Why does what I learned today matter? How do I implement it in my life today? How should my perspective change based on what I have learned? Look for applications that affect your relationship to God, with others, and your view of self. Use the space below to explore these questions.

ENCOURAGE

How I can share what I have learned to help someone else?

When do I plan to share this? Who do I plan to sharing this with? How do I plan to share this? In-person? Text message? Phone call? Social Media? Use the space below to develop a plan of action.

_____
_____
_____
_____
_____
_____
_____
_____
_____
_____
_____
_____
_____
_____
_____
_____
_____
_____
_____
_____
_____
_____
_____
_____
_____

Additional Notes:

How to Study the Bible
The **H.U.S.T.L.E.** Way

H — **HUMBLE**
Humble yourself and pray.

U — **UNDERSTAND**
Look up different translations, definitions and cross references.

S — **STUDY**
What is the text saying to me?

T — **TUNE IN**
Relax, let go, be quiet before the Lord and listen.

L — **LIVE**
How can you apply this Word to your life?

E — **ENCOURAGE**
How I can share what I have learned to help someone else?

Date:

HUMBLE
yourself and pray.

James 1:5, KJV:
"If any of you lack wisdom, let him ask of God, that giveth to all men liberally, and upbraideth not; and it shall be given him."

Lord, thank You for this time You've given me to open Your Word and discover who You are. Thank You that You don't leave us in the dark about who You are and what You are doing in the world, but that You have revealed Yourself and Your Will through the Bible, Your sacred Words to us.

Lord, I need wisdom as I read Your Word. You promise us in James 1:5 that we only have to ask for wisdom to receive it. Lord, please give me Your wisdom now as I approach Your Word. Help me discern the truth of this text. Help me not rely on my own understanding. Thank you God for the clarity, encouragement and hope Your Word brings.

In Jesus' Name I pray, Amen.

Use the space below to pray specifically about what you would like God to reveal through your Bible Study.

Dear Heavenly Father:

_____
_____
_____
_____
_____
_____
_____
_____
_____
_____
_____
_____
_____
_____
_____
_____
_____
_____
_____
_____
_____
_____
_____
_____
_____
_____

In Jesus Name I pray, Amen

UNDERSTAND
Look up different translations, definitions and cross references.

Scripture: _____

Use the space below to write out the scripture in your favorite translation, then choose another translation to write the scripture out.

Favorite Translation:

_____
_____
_____
_____
_____
_____
_____
_____
_____
_____

Another Translation:

_____
_____
_____
_____
_____
_____
_____
_____
_____
_____

Note any words that are different between the two translations. Use a Bible Dictionary to look up the words. Also read the cross-reference scriptures to dive deeper into the scripture and gain a better understanding.

UNDERSTAND

Words that stand out/are different per translation:

_____
_____
_____
_____
_____
_____
_____

Definitions:

_____
_____
_____
_____
_____
_____
_____
_____
_____

Cross-Reference Scriptures:

_____
_____
_____
_____
_____
_____
_____
_____
_____

STUDY

What is the text saying to me?

Use the S.P.E.C.K. Method to explore the text.

S.IN TO CONFESS + AVOID

In the passage, does God say something about sin? Is there a sin to confess? Is there a sin that I should avoid?

P.ROMISE TO KEEP

Does God communicate a promise for me to claim?

E.XAMPLE TO FOLLOW

Do I find role models in this passage? What character traits and which actions are commendable? Which are not?

C.OMMAND TO OBEY

Are there any specific commands given for me to follow. What does God want me to apply to my life today and this week so that I develop Godly character and habits?

K. – KNOWLEDGE ABOUT GOD

What does this passage tell me about God or about Jesus Christ or the Holy Spirit? What is God like? What are His attributes? What does He do? What does He like and dislike? What is His attitude?

NOTE - you can't always answer all 5 parts.

STUDY

S. in to confess + avoid

_____
_____
_____
_____
_____
_____

P. romise to keep

_____
_____
_____
_____
_____
_____
_____
_____

E. xample to follow

_____
_____
_____
_____
_____
_____
_____
_____

STUDY

C. ommand to obey

_____
_____
_____
_____
_____
_____
_____
_____
_____
_____

K. nowledge about God

_____
_____
_____
_____
_____
_____
_____
_____
_____
_____
_____
_____
_____
_____

TUNE IN

Relax, let go, be quiet before the Lord and listen.

This is a time of focus. Focus on the scripture and set your mind on the Father, Son, and Holy Spirit. Take as much time as you need. Don't rush this part! After some time has passed, use the space below to write anything God revealed or spoke to you.

_____
_____
_____
_____
_____
_____
_____
_____
_____
_____
_____
_____
_____
_____
_____
_____
_____
_____
_____
_____
_____
_____
_____
_____
_____

LIVE

How can you apply this Word to your life?

Why does what I learned today matter? How do I implement it in my life today? How should my perspective change based on what I have learned? Look for applications that affect your relationship to God, with others, and your view of self. Use the space below to explore these questions.

ENCOURAGE

How I can share what I have learned to help someone else?

When do I plan to share this? Who do I plan to sharing this with? How do I plan to share this? In-person? Text message? Phone call? Social Media? Use the space below to develop a plan of action.

_____
_____
_____
_____
_____
_____
_____
_____
_____
_____
_____
_____
_____
_____
_____
_____
_____
_____
_____
_____
_____
_____
_____
_____
_____

Additional Notes:

How to Study the Bible
The H.U.S.T.L.E. Way

H — **HUMBLE**
Humble yourself and pray.

U — **UNDERSTAND**
Look up different translations, definitions and cross references.

S — **STUDY**
What is the text saying to me?

T — **TUNE IN**
Relax, let go, be quiet before the Lord and listen.

L — **LIVE**
How can you apply this Word to your life?

E — **ENCOURAGE**
How I can share what I have learned to help someone else?

Date:

HUMBLE
yourself and pray.

James 1:5, KJV:
"If any of you lack wisdom, let him ask of God, that giveth to all men liberally, and upbraideth not; and it shall be given him."

Lord, thank You for this time You've given me to open Your Word and discover who You are. Thank You that You don't leave us in the dark about who You are and what You are doing in the world, but that You have revealed Yourself and Your Will through the Bible, Your sacred Words to us.

Lord, I need wisdom as I read Your Word. You promise us in James 1:5 that we only have to ask for wisdom to receive it. Lord, please give me Your wisdom now as I approach Your Word. Help me discern the truth of this text. Help me not rely on my own understanding. Thank you God for the clarity, encouragement and hope Your Word brings.

In Jesus' Name I pray, Amen.

Use the space below to pray specifically about what you would like God to reveal through your Bible Study.

Dear Heavenly Father:

_____
_____
_____
_____
_____
_____
_____
_____
_____
_____
_____
_____
_____
_____
_____
_____
_____
_____
_____
_____
_____
_____
_____
_____
_____

In Jesus Name I pray, Amen

UNDERSTAND
Look up different translations, definitions and cross references.

Scripture: _____

Use the space below to write out the scripture in your favorite translation, then choose another translation to write the scripture out.

Favorite Translation:
_____
_____
_____
_____
_____
_____
_____
_____

Another Translation:
_____
_____
_____
_____
_____
_____
_____
_____

Note any words that are different between the two translations. Use a Bible Dictionary to look up the words. Also read the cross-reference scriptures to dive deeper into the scripture and gain a better understanding.

Study H.U.S.T.L.E. Repeat

UNDERSTAND

Words that stand out/are different per translation:

_____
_____
_____
_____
_____
_____
_____

Definitions:

_____
_____
_____
_____
_____
_____
_____

Cross-Reference Scriptures:

_____
_____
_____
_____
_____
_____
_____

STUDY

What is the text saying to me?

Use the S.P.E.C.K. Method to explore the text.

S.IN TO CONFESS + AVOID

In the passage, does God say something about sin? Is there a sin to confess? Is there a sin that I should avoid?

P.ROMISE TO KEEP

Does God communicate a promise for me to claim?

E.XAMPLE TO FOLLOW

Do I find role models in this passage? What character traits and which actions are commendable? Which are not?

C.OMMAND TO OBEY

Are there any specific commands given for me to follow. What does God want me to apply to my life today and this week so that I develop Godly character and habits?

K. – KNOWLEDGE ABOUT GOD

What does this passage tell me about God or about Jesus Christ or the Holy Spirit? What is God like? What are His attributes? What does He do? What does He like and dislike? What is His attitude?

NOTE - you can't always answer all 5 parts.

STUDY

S. in to confess + avoid

_____
_____
_____
_____
_____
_____
_____

P. romise to keep

_____
_____
_____
_____
_____
_____
_____
_____

E. xample to follow

_____
_____
_____
_____
_____
_____
_____
_____

Study H.U.S.T.L.E. Repeat

STUDY

C. ommand to obey

_____
_____
_____
_____
_____
_____
_____
_____
_____
_____
_____
_____

K. nowledge about God

_____
_____
_____
_____
_____
_____
_____
_____
_____
_____
_____
_____
_____
_____
_____
_____

TUNE IN

Relax, let go, be quiet before the Lord and listen.

This is a time of focus. Focus on the scripture and set your mind on the Father, Son, and Holy Spirit. Take as much time as you need. Don't rush this part! After some time has passed, use the space below to write anything God revealed or spoke to you.

_____
_____
_____
_____
_____
_____
_____
_____
_____
_____
_____
_____
_____
_____
_____
_____
_____
_____
_____
_____
_____
_____
_____
_____
_____

LIVE

How can you apply this Word to your life?

Why does what I learned today matter? How do I implement it in my life today? How should my perspective change based on what I have learned? Look for applications that affect your relationship to God, with others, and your view of self. Use the space below to explore these questions.

_____
_____
_____
_____
_____
_____
_____
_____
_____
_____
_____
_____
_____
_____
_____
_____
_____
_____
_____
_____
_____
_____
_____
_____
_____

ENCOURAGE

How I can share what I have learned to help someone else?

When do I plan to share this? Who do I plan to sharing this with? How do I plan to share this? In-person? Text message? Phone call? Social Media? Use the space below to develop a plan of action.

_____
_____
_____
_____
_____
_____
_____
_____
_____
_____
_____
_____
_____
_____
_____
_____
_____
_____
_____
_____
_____
_____
_____
_____
_____
_____

Additional Notes:

How to Study the Bible
The **H.U.S.T.L.E.** Way

H

HUMBLE
Humble yourself and pray.

U

UNDERSTAND
Look up different translations, definitions and cross references.

S

STUDY
What is the text saying to me?

T

TUNE IN
Relax, let go, be quiet before the Lord and listen.

L

LIVE
How can you apply this Word to your life?

E

ENCOURAGE
How I can share what I have learned to help someone else?

Date:

HUMBLE
yourself and pray.

James 1:5, KJV:
"If any of you lack wisdom, let him ask of God, that giveth to all men liberally, and upbraideth not; and it shall be given him."

Lord, thank You for this time You've given me to open Your Word and discover who You are. Thank You that You don't leave us in the dark about who You are and what You are doing in the world, but that You have revealed Yourself and Your Will through the Bible, Your sacred Words to us.

Lord, I need wisdom as I read Your Word. You promise us in James 1:5 that we only have to ask for wisdom to receive it. Lord, please give me Your wisdom now as I approach Your Word. Help me discern the truth of this text. Help me not rely on my own understanding. Thank you God for the clarity, encouragement and hope Your Word brings.

In Jesus' Name I pray, Amen.

Use the space below to pray specifically about what you would like God to reveal through your Bible Study.

Dear Heavenly Father:

_____

In Jesus Name I pray, Amen

UNDERSTAND

Look up different translations, definitions and cross references.

Scripture: _____

Use the space below to write out the scripture in your favorite translation, then choose another translation to write the scripture out.

Favorite Translation:

_____
_____
_____
_____
_____
_____
_____
_____

Another Translation:

_____
_____
_____
_____
_____
_____
_____
_____

Note any words that are different between the two translations. Use a Bible Dictionary to look up the words. Also read the cross-reference scriptures to dive deeper into the scripture and gain a better understanding.

UNDERSTAND

Words that stand out/are different per translation:

_____
_____
_____
_____
_____
_____
_____
_____

Definitions:

_____
_____
_____
_____
_____
_____
_____
_____

Cross-Reference Scriptures:

_____
_____
_____
_____
_____
_____
_____
_____

STUDY

What is the text saying to me?

Use the S.P.E.C.K. Method to explore the text.

S.IN TO CONFESS + AVOID

In the passage, does God say something about sin? Is there a sin to confess? Is there a sin that I should avoid?

P.ROMISE TO KEEP

Does God communicate a promise for me to claim?

E.XAMPLE TO FOLLOW

Do I find role models in this passage? What character traits and which actions are commendable? Which are not?

C.OMMAND TO OBEY

Are there any specific commands given for me to follow. What does God want me to apply to my life today and this week so that I develop Godly character and habits?

K. – KNOWLEDGE ABOUT GOD

What does this passage tell me about God or about Jesus Christ or the Holy Spirit? What is God like? What are His attributes? What does He do? What does He like and dislike? What is His attitude?

NOTE - you can't always answer all 5 parts.

STUDY

S. in to confess + avoid

_____
_____
_____
_____
_____
_____

P. romise to keep

_____
_____
_____
_____
_____
_____

E. xample to follow

_____
_____
_____
_____
_____
_____

STUDY

C. ommand to obey

_____
_____
_____
_____
_____
_____
_____
_____
_____

K. nowledge about God

_____
_____
_____
_____
_____
_____
_____
_____
_____
_____
_____
_____
_____
_____
_____

TUNE IN

Relax, let go, be quiet before the Lord and listen.

This is a time of focus. Focus on the scripture and set your mind on the Father, Son, and Holy Spirit. Take as much time as you need. Don't rush this part! After some time has passed, use the space below to write anything God revealed or spoke to you.

_____
_____
_____
_____
_____
_____
_____
_____
_____
_____
_____
_____
_____
_____
_____
_____
_____
_____
_____
_____
_____
_____
_____
_____

LIVE

How can you apply this Word to your life?

Why does what I learned today matter? How do I implement it in my life today? How should my perspective change based on what I have learned? Look for applications that affect your relationship to God, with others, and your view of self. Use the space below to explore these questions.

_____
_____
_____
_____
_____
_____
_____
_____
_____
_____
_____
_____
_____
_____
_____
_____
_____
_____
_____
_____
_____
_____
_____
_____
_____

ENCOURAGE

How I can share what I have learned to help someone else?

When do I plan to share this? Who do I plan to sharing this with? How do I plan to share this? In-person? Text message? Phone call? Social Media? Use the space below to develop a plan of action.

Additional Notes:

Study H.U.S.T.L.E. Repeat

How to Study the Bible
The H.U.S.T.L.E. Way

H — HUMBLE
Humble yourself and pray.

U — UNDERSTAND
Look up different translations, definitions and cross references.

S — STUDY
What is the text saying to me?

T — TUNE IN
Relax, let go, be quiet before the Lord and listen.

L — LIVE
How can you apply this Word to your life?

E — ENCOURAGE
How I can share what I have learned to help someone else?

The H.U.S.T.L.E. Bible Study Method

Date:

HUMBLE
yourself and pray.

James 1:5, KJV:
"If any of you lack wisdom, let him ask of God, that giveth to all men liberally, and upbraideth not; and it shall be given him."

Lord, thank You for this time You've given me to open Your Word and discover who You are. Thank You that You don't leave us in the dark about who You are and what You are doing in the world, but that You have revealed Yourself and Your Will through the Bible, Your sacred Words to us.

Lord, I need wisdom as I read Your Word. You promise us in James 1:5 that we only have to ask for wisdom to receive it. Lord, please give me Your wisdom now as I approach Your Word. Help me discern the truth of this text. Help me not rely on my own understanding. Thank you God for the clarity, encouragement and hope Your Word brings.

In Jesus' Name I pray, Amen.

Use the space below to pray specifically about what you would like God to reveal through your Bible Study.

Dear Heavenly Father:

_____
_____
_____
_____
_____
_____
_____
_____
_____
_____
_____
_____
_____
_____
_____
_____
_____
_____
_____
_____
_____
_____
_____
_____
_____
_____
_____

In Jesus Name I pray, Amen

UNDERSTAND

Look up different translations, definitions and cross references.

Scripture: _____

Use the space below to write out the scripture in your favorite translation, then choose another translation to write the scripture out.

Favorite Translation:

_____
_____
_____
_____
_____
_____
_____
_____
_____

Another Translation:

_____
_____
_____
_____
_____
_____
_____
_____
_____

Note any words that are different between the two translations. Use a Bible Dictionary to look up the words. Also read the cross-reference scriptures to dive deeper into the scripture and gain a better understanding.

UNDERSTAND

Words that stand out/are different per translation:

_____
_____
_____
_____
_____
_____
_____

Definitions:

_____
_____
_____
_____
_____
_____
_____

Cross-Reference Scriptures:

_____
_____
_____
_____
_____
_____
_____

STUDY

What is the text saying to me?

Use the S.P.E.C.K. Method to explore the text.

S.IN TO CONFESS + AVOID

In the passage, does God say something about sin? Is there a sin to confess? Is there a sin that I should avoid?

P.ROMISE TO KEEP

Does God communicate a promise for me to claim?

E.XAMPLE TO FOLLOW

Do I find role models in this passage? What character traits and which actions are commendable? Which are not?

C.OMMAND TO OBEY

Are there any specific commands given for me to follow. What does God want me to apply to my life today and this week so that I develop Godly character and habits?

K. – KNOWLEDGE ABOUT GOD

What does this passage tell me about God or about Jesus Christ or the Holy Spirit? What is God like? What are His attributes? What does He do? What does He like and dislike? What is His attitude?

NOTE - you can't always answer all 5 parts.

STUDY

S. in to confess + avoid

_____
_____
_____
_____
_____
_____

P. romise to keep

_____
_____
_____
_____
_____
_____

E. xample to follow

_____
_____
_____
_____
_____
_____

STUDY

C. ommand to obey

_____
_____
_____
_____
_____
_____
_____
_____
_____

K. nowledge about God

_____
_____
_____
_____
_____
_____
_____
_____
_____
_____
_____
_____
_____
_____
_____
_____
_____

TUNE IN

Relax, let go, be quiet before the Lord and listen.

This is a time of focus. Focus on the scripture and set your mind on the Father, Son, and Holy Spirit. Take as much time as you need. Don't rush this part! After some time has passed, use the space below to write anything God revealed or spoke to you.

_____
_____
_____
_____
_____
_____
_____
_____
_____
_____
_____
_____
_____
_____
_____
_____
_____
_____
_____
_____
_____
_____
_____
_____

LIVE

How can you apply this Word to your life?

Why does what I learned today matter? How do I implement it in my life today? How should my perspective change based on what I have learned? Look for applications that affect your relationship to God, with others, and your view of self. Use the space below to explore these questions.

ENCOURAGE
How I can share what I have learned to help someone else?

When do I plan to share this? Who do I plan to sharing this with? How do I plan to share this? In-person? Text message? Phone call? Social Media? Use the space below to develop a plan of action.

_____
_____
_____
_____
_____
_____
_____
_____
_____
_____
_____
_____
_____
_____
_____
_____
_____
_____
_____
_____
_____
_____
_____
_____
_____
_____

Additional Notes:

How to Study the Bible
The H.U.S.T.L.E. Way

H — **HUMBLE**
Humble yourself and pray.

U — **UNDERSTAND**
Look up different translations, definitions and cross references.

S — **STUDY**
What is the text saying to me?

T — **TUNE IN**
Relax, let go, be quiet before the Lord and listen.

L — **LIVE**
How can you apply this Word to your life?

E — **ENCOURAGE**
How I can share what I have learned to help someone else?

The H.U.S.T.L.E. Bible Study Method

Date:

HUMBLE
yourself and pray.

James 1:5, KJV:
"If any of you lack wisdom, let him ask of God, that giveth to all men liberally, and upbraideth not; and it shall be given him."

Lord, thank You for this time You've given me to open Your Word and discover who You are. Thank You that You don't leave us in the dark about who You are and what You are doing in the world, but that You have revealed Yourself and Your Will through the Bible, Your sacred Words to us.

Lord, I need wisdom as I read Your Word. You promise us in James 1:5 that we only have to ask for wisdom to receive it. Lord, please give me Your wisdom now as I approach Your Word. Help me discern the truth of this text. Help me not rely on my own understanding. Thank you God for the clarity, encouragement and hope Your Word brings.

In Jesus' Name I pray, Amen.

Use the space below to pray specifically about what you would like God to reveal through your Bible Study.

Dear Heavenly Father:

_____
_____
_____
_____
_____
_____
_____
_____
_____
_____
_____
_____
_____
_____
_____
_____
_____
_____
_____
_____
_____
_____
_____
_____
_____
_____

In Jesus Name I pray, Amen

UNDERSTAND
Look up different translations, definitions and cross references.

Scripture: _____

Use the space below to write out the scripture in your favorite translation, then choose another translation to write the scripture out.

Favorite Translation:
_____
_____
_____
_____
_____
_____
_____
_____

Another Translation:
_____
_____
_____
_____
_____
_____
_____
_____

Note any words that are different between the two translations. Use a Bible Dictionary to look up the words. Also read the cross-reference scriptures to dive deeper into the scripture and gain a better understanding.

UNDERSTAND

Words that stand out/are different per translation:

_____
_____
_____
_____
_____
_____
_____
_____

Definitions:

_____
_____
_____
_____
_____
_____
_____
_____
_____

Cross-Reference Scriptures:

_____
_____
_____
_____
_____
_____
_____
_____
_____

STUDY

What is the text saying to me?

Use the S.P.E.C.K. Method to explore the text.

S.IN TO CONFESS + AVOID

In the passage, does God say something about sin? Is there a sin to confess? Is there a sin that I should avoid?

P.ROMISE TO KEEP

Does God communicate a promise for me to claim?

E.XAMPLE TO FOLLOW

Do I find role models in this passage? What character traits and which actions are commendable? Which are not?

C.OMMAND TO OBEY

Are there any specific commands given for me to follow. What does God want me to apply to my life today and this week so that I develop Godly character and habits?

K. – KNOWLEDGE ABOUT GOD

What does this passage tell me about God or about Jesus Christ or the Holy Spirit? What is God like? What are His attributes? What does He do? What does He like and dislike? What is His attitude?

NOTE - you can't always answer all 5 parts.

STUDY

S. in to confess + avoid

_____
_____
_____
_____
_____
_____

P. romise to keep

_____
_____
_____
_____
_____
_____
_____
_____

E. xample to follow

_____
_____
_____
_____
_____
_____
_____
_____

STUDY

C. ommand to obey

_____
_____
_____
_____
_____
_____
_____
_____

K. nowledge about God

_____
_____
_____
_____
_____
_____
_____
_____
_____
_____
_____
_____
_____
_____

TUNE IN

Relax, let go, be quiet before the Lord and listen.

This is a time of focus. Focus on the scripture and set your mind on the Father, Son, and Holy Spirit. Take as much time as you need. Don't rush this part! After some time has passed, use the space below to write anything God revealed or spoke to you.

_____
_____
_____
_____
_____
_____
_____
_____
_____
_____
_____
_____
_____
_____
_____
_____
_____
_____
_____
_____
_____
_____
_____
_____
_____
_____
_____

LIVE

How can you apply this Word to your life?

Why does what I learned today matter? How do I implement it in my life today? How should my perspective change based on what I have learned? Look for applications that affect your relationship to God, with others, and your view of self. Use the space below to explore these questions.

ENCOURAGE

How I can share what I have learned to help someone else?

When do I plan to share this? Who do I plan to sharing this with? How do I plan to share this? In-person? Text message? Phone call? Social Media? Use the space below to develop a plan of action.

_____
_____
_____
_____
_____
_____
_____
_____
_____
_____
_____
_____
_____
_____
_____
_____
_____
_____
_____
_____
_____
_____
_____
_____
_____
_____
_____
_____

Additional Notes:

_____
_____
_____
_____
_____
_____
_____
_____
_____
_____
_____
_____
_____
_____
_____
_____
_____
_____
_____
_____
_____
_____
_____
_____
_____
_____
_____
_____

Study H.U.S.T.L.E. Repeat

How to Study the Bible
The H.U.S.T.L.E. Way

H

HUMBLE
Humble yourself and pray.

U

UNDERSTAND
Look up different translations, definitions and cross references.

S

STUDY
What is the text saying to me?

T

TUNE IN
Relax, let go, be quiet before the Lord and listen.

L

LIVE
How can you apply this Word to your life?

E

ENCOURAGE
How I can share what I have learned to help someone else?

The H.U.S.T.L.E. Bible Study Method

Date:

HUMBLE
yourself and pray.

James 1:5, KJV:
"If any of you lack wisdom, let him ask of God, that giveth to all men liberally, and upbraideth not; and it shall be given him."

Lord, thank You for this time You've given me to open Your Word and discover who You are. Thank You that You don't leave us in the dark about who You are and what You are doing in the world, but that You have revealed Yourself and Your Will through the Bible, Your sacred Words to us.

Lord, I need wisdom as I read Your Word. You promise us in James 1:5 that we only have to ask for wisdom to receive it. Lord, please give me Your wisdom now as I approach Your Word. Help me discern the truth of this text. Help me not rely on my own understanding. Thank you God for the clarity, encouragement and hope Your Word brings.

In Jesus' Name I pray, Amen.

Use the space below to pray specifically about what you would like God to reveal through your Bible Study.

Dear Heavenly Father:

_____
_____
_____
_____
_____
_____
_____
_____
_____
_____
_____
_____
_____
_____
_____
_____
_____
_____
_____
_____
_____
_____
_____
_____
_____

In Jesus Name I pray, Amen

UNDERSTAND
Look up different translations, definitions and cross references.

Scripture: _____

Use the space below to write out the scripture in your favorite translation, then choose another translation to write the scripture out.

Favorite Translation:

_____
_____
_____
_____
_____
_____
_____
_____
_____

Another Translation:

_____
_____
_____
_____
_____
_____
_____
_____
_____

Note any words that are different between the two translations. Use a Bible Dictionary to look up the words. Also read the cross-reference scriptures to dive deeper into the scripture and gain a better understanding.

UNDERSTAND

Words that stand out/are different per translation:

_____
_____
_____
_____
_____
_____
_____

Definitions:

_____
_____
_____
_____
_____
_____
_____

Cross-Reference Scriptures:

_____
_____
_____
_____
_____
_____
_____

STUDY

What is the text saying to me?

Use the S.P.E.C.K. Method to explore the text.

S.IN TO CONFESS + AVOID

In the passage, does God say something about sin? Is there a sin to confess? Is there a sin that I should avoid?

P.ROMISE TO KEEP

Does God communicate a promise for me to claim?

E.XAMPLE TO FOLLOW

Do I find role models in this passage? What character traits and which actions are commendable? Which are not?

C.OMMAND TO OBEY

Are there any specific commands given for me to follow. What does God want me to apply to my life today and this week so that I develop Godly character and habits?

K. – KNOWLEDGE ABOUT GOD

What does this passage tell me about God or about Jesus Christ or the Holy Spirit? What is God like? What are His attributes? What does He do? What does He like and dislike? What is His attitude?

NOTE - you can't always answer all 5 parts.

STUDY

S. in to confess + avoid

_____
_____
_____
_____
_____
_____

P. romise to keep

_____
_____
_____
_____
_____
_____
_____

E. xample to follow

_____
_____
_____
_____
_____
_____
_____

STUDY

C. ommand to obey

_____
_____
_____
_____
_____
_____
_____
_____
_____

K. nowledge about God

_____
_____
_____
_____
_____
_____
_____
_____
_____
_____
_____
_____
_____
_____
_____

TUNE IN

Relax, let go, be quiet before the Lord and listen.

This is a time of focus. Focus on the scripture and set your mind on the Father, Son, and Holy Spirit. Take as much time as you need. Don't rush this part! After some time has passed, use the space below to write anything God revealed or spoke to you.

_____
_____
_____
_____
_____
_____
_____
_____
_____
_____
_____
_____
_____
_____
_____
_____
_____
_____
_____
_____
_____
_____
_____
_____
_____

LIVE

How can you apply this Word to your life?

Why does what I learned today matter? How do I implement it in my life today? How should my perspective change based on what I have learned? Look for applications that affect your relationship to God, with others, and your view of self. Use the space below to explore these questions.

ENCOURAGE

How I can share what I have learned to help someone else?

When do I plan to share this? Who do I plan to sharing this with? How do I plan to share this? In-person? Text message? Phone call? Social Media? Use the space below to develop a plan of action.

_____
_____
_____
_____
_____
_____
_____
_____
_____
_____
_____
_____
_____
_____
_____
_____
_____
_____
_____
_____
_____
_____
_____
_____
_____

Additional Notes:

How to Study the Bible
The **H.U.S.T.L.E.** Way

H — **HUMBLE**
Humble yourself and pray.

U — **UNDERSTAND**
Look up different translations, definitions and cross references.

S — **STUDY**
What is the text saying to me?

T — **TUNE IN**
Relax, let go, be quiet before the Lord and listen.

L — **LIVE**
How can you apply this Word to your life?

E — **ENCOURAGE**
How I can share what I have learned to help someone else?

The H.U.S.T.L.E. Bible Study Method

Date:

HUMBLE
yourself and pray.

James 1:5, KJV:
"If any of you lack wisdom, let him ask of God, that giveth to all men liberally, and upbraideth not; and it shall be given him."

Lord, thank You for this time You've given me to open Your Word and discover who You are. Thank You that You don't leave us in the dark about who You are and what You are doing in the world, but that You have revealed Yourself and Your Will through the Bible, Your sacred Words to us.

Lord, I need wisdom as I read Your Word. You promise us in James 1:5 that we only have to ask for wisdom to receive it. Lord, please give me Your wisdom now as I approach Your Word. Help me discern the truth of this text. Help me not rely on my own understanding. Thank you God for the clarity, encouragement and hope Your Word brings.

In Jesus' Name I pray, Amen.

Use the space below to pray specifically about what you would like God to reveal through your Bible Study.

Dear Heavenly Father:

_____
_____
_____
_____
_____
_____
_____
_____
_____
_____
_____
_____
_____
_____
_____
_____
_____
_____
_____
_____
_____
_____
_____
_____
_____
_____
_____
_____
_____
_____

In Jesus Name I pray, Amen

UNDERSTAND
Look up different translations, definitions and cross references.

Scripture: _____

Use the space below to write out the scripture in your favorite translation, then choose another translation to write the scripture out.

Favorite Translation:

_____
_____
_____
_____
_____
_____
_____
_____
_____
_____

Another Translation:

_____
_____
_____
_____
_____
_____
_____
_____
_____
_____

Note any words that are different between the two translations. Use a Bible Dictionary to look up the words. Also read the cross-reference scriptures to dive deeper into the scripture and gain a better understanding.

UNDERSTAND

Words that stand out/are different per translation:

_____
_____
_____
_____
_____
_____
_____

Definitions:

_____
_____
_____
_____
_____
_____
_____
_____

Cross-Reference Scriptures:

_____
_____
_____
_____
_____
_____
_____
_____

STUDY

What is the text saying to me?

Use the S.P.E.C.K. Method to explore the text.

S.IN TO CONFESS + AVOID

In the passage, does God say something about sin? Is there a sin to confess? Is there a sin that I should avoid?

P.ROMISE TO KEEP

Does God communicate a promise for me to claim?

E.XAMPLE TO FOLLOW

Do I find role models in this passage? What character traits and which actions are commendable? Which are not?

C.OMMAND TO OBEY

Are there any specific commands given for me to follow. What does God want me to apply to my life today and this week so that I develop Godly character and habits?

K. – KNOWLEDGE ABOUT GOD

What does this passage tell me about God or about Jesus Christ or the Holy Spirit? What is God like? What are His attributes? What does He do? What does He like and dislike? What is His attitude?

NOTE - you can't always answer all 5 parts.

STUDY

S. in to confess + avoid

_____
_____
_____
_____
_____
_____

P. romise to keep

_____
_____
_____
_____
_____
_____

E. xample to follow

_____
_____
_____
_____
_____
_____

STUDY

C. ommand to obey

_____
_____
_____
_____
_____
_____
_____
_____
_____
_____
_____
_____

K. nowledge about God

_____
_____
_____
_____
_____
_____
_____
_____
_____
_____
_____
_____
_____
_____
_____
_____

TUNE IN

Relax, let go, be quiet before the Lord and listen.

This is a time of focus. Focus on the scripture and set your mind on the Father, Son, and Holy Spirit. Take as much time as you need. Don't rush this part! After some time has passed, use the space below to write anything God revealed or spoke to you.

_____
_____
_____
_____
_____
_____
_____
_____
_____
_____
_____
_____
_____
_____
_____
_____
_____
_____
_____
_____
_____
_____
_____
_____

LIVE

How can you apply this Word to your life?

Why does what I learned today matter? How do I implement it in my life today? How should my perspective change based on what I have learned? Look for applications that affect your relationship to God, with others, and your view of self. Use the space below to explore these questions.

_____
_____
_____
_____
_____
_____
_____
_____
_____
_____
_____
_____
_____
_____
_____
_____
_____
_____
_____
_____
_____
_____
_____
_____

ENCOURAGE

How I can share what I have learned to help someone else?

When do I plan to share this? Who do I plan to sharing this with? How do I plan to share this? In-person? Text message? Phone call? Social Media? Use the space below to develop a plan of action.

_____
_____
_____
_____
_____
_____
_____
_____
_____
_____
_____
_____
_____
_____
_____
_____
_____
_____
_____
_____
_____
_____
_____
_____
_____

Additional Notes:

Study H.U.S.T.L.E. Repeat

How to Study the Bible
The **H.U.S.T.L.E.** Way

H — **HUMBLE**
Humble yourself and pray.

U — **UNDERSTAND**
Look up different translations, definitions and cross references.

S — **STUDY**
What is the text saying to me?

T — **TUNE IN**
Relax, let go, be quiet before the Lord and listen.

L — **LIVE**
How can you apply this Word to your life?

E — **ENCOURAGE**
How I can share what I have learned to help someone else?

The H.U.S.T.L.E. Bible Study Method

Date:

HUMBLE
yourself and pray.

James 1:5, KJV:
"If any of you lack wisdom, let him ask of God, that giveth to all men liberally, and upbraideth not; and it shall be given him."

Lord, thank You for this time You've given me to open Your Word and discover who You are. Thank You that You don't leave us in the dark about who You are and what You are doing in the world, but that You have revealed Yourself and Your Will through the Bible, Your sacred Words to us.

Lord, I need wisdom as I read Your Word. You promise us in James 1:5 that we only have to ask for wisdom to receive it. Lord, please give me Your wisdom now as I approach Your Word. Help me discern the truth of this text. Help me not rely on my own understanding. Thank you God for the clarity, encouragement and hope Your Word brings.

In Jesus' Name I pray, Amen.

Use the space below to pray specifically about what you would like God to reveal through your Bible Study.

Dear Heavenly Father:

In Jesus Name I pray, Amen

UNDERSTAND
Look up different translations, definitions and cross references.

Scripture: _____

Use the space below to write out the scripture in your favorite translation, then choose another translation to write the scripture out.

Favorite Translation:

_____
_____
_____
_____
_____
_____
_____
_____

Another Translation:

_____
_____
_____
_____
_____
_____
_____
_____

Note any words that are different between the two translations. Use a Bible Dictionary to look up the words. Also read the cross-reference scriptures to dive deeper into the scripture and gain a better understanding.

UNDERSTAND

Words that stand out/are different per translation:
_____
_____
_____
_____
_____
_____
_____

Definitions:
_____
_____
_____
_____
_____
_____
_____

Cross-Reference Scriptures:
_____
_____
_____
_____
_____
_____
_____

STUDY

What is the text saying to me?

Use the S.P.E.C.K. Method to explore the text.

S.IN TO CONFESS + AVOID

In the passage, does God say something about sin? Is there a sin to confess? Is there a sin that I should avoid?

P.ROMISE TO KEEP

Does God communicate a promise for me to claim?

E.XAMPLE TO FOLLOW

Do I find role models in this passage? What character traits and which actions are commendable? Which are not?

C.OMMAND TO OBEY

Are there any specific commands given for me to follow. What does God want me to apply to my life today and this week so that I develop Godly character and habits?

K. – KNOWLEDGE ABOUT GOD

What does this passage tell me about God or about Jesus Christ or the Holy Spirit? What is God like? What are His attributes? What does He do? What does He like and dislike? What is His attitude?

NOTE - you can't always answer all 5 parts.

STUDY

S. in to confess + avoid

_____
_____
_____
_____
_____
_____

P. romise to keep

_____
_____
_____
_____
_____
_____

E. xample to follow

_____
_____
_____
_____
_____
_____

STUDY

C. ommand to obey

_____
_____
_____
_____
_____
_____
_____
_____
_____

K. nowledge about God

_____
_____
_____
_____
_____
_____
_____
_____
_____
_____
_____
_____
_____
_____
_____

TUNE IN

Relax, let go, be quiet before the Lord and listen.

This is a time of focus. Focus on the scripture and set your mind on the Father, Son, and Holy Spirit. Take as much time as you need. Don't rush this part! After some time has passed, use the space below to write anything God revealed or spoke to you.

_____
_____
_____
_____
_____
_____
_____
_____
_____
_____
_____
_____
_____
_____
_____
_____
_____
_____
_____
_____
_____
_____
_____
_____
_____
_____

LIVE

How can you apply this Word to your life?

Why does what I learned today matter? How do I implement it in my life today? How should my perspective change based on what I have learned? Look for applications that affect your relationship to God, with others, and your view of self. Use the space below to explore these questions.

_____
_____
_____
_____
_____
_____
_____
_____
_____
_____
_____
_____
_____
_____
_____
_____
_____
_____
_____
_____
_____
_____
_____
_____
_____

ENCOURAGE

How I can share what I have learned to help someone else?

When do I plan to share this? Who do I plan to sharing this with? How do I plan to share this? In-person? Text message? Phone call? Social Media? Use the space below to develop a plan of action.

Additional Notes:

Study H.U.S.T.L.E. Repeat

Date:

HUMBLE
yourself and pray.

James 1:5, KJV:
"If any of you lack wisdom, let him ask of God, that giveth to all men liberally, and upbraideth not; and it shall be given him."

Lord, thank You for this time You've given me to open Your Word and discover who You are. Thank You that You don't leave us in the dark about who You are and what You are doing in the world, but that You have revealed Yourself and Your Will through the Bible, Your sacred Words to us.

Lord, I need wisdom as I read Your Word. You promise us in James 1:5 that we only have to ask for wisdom to receive it. Lord, please give me Your wisdom now as I approach Your Word. Help me discern the truth of this text. Help me not rely on my own understanding. Thank you God for the clarity, encouragement and hope Your Word brings.

In Jesus' Name I pray, Amen.

Use the space below to pray specifically about what you would like God to reveal through your Bible Study.

Dear Heavenly Father:

_____
_____
_____
_____
_____
_____
_____
_____
_____
_____
_____
_____
_____
_____
_____
_____
_____
_____
_____
_____
_____
_____
_____
_____
_____
_____
_____
_____
_____
_____

In Jesus Name I pray, Amen

UNDERSTAND
Look up different translations, definitions and cross references.

Scripture: _____

Use the space below to write out the scripture in your favorite translation, then choose another translation to write the scripture out.

Favorite Translation:
_____
_____
_____
_____
_____
_____
_____
_____

Another Translation:
_____
_____
_____
_____
_____
_____
_____
_____

Note any words that are different between the two translations. Use a Bible Dictionary to look up the words. Also read the cross-reference scriptures to dive deeper into the scripture and gain a better understanding.

UNDERSTAND

Words that stand out/are different per translation:

_____
_____
_____
_____
_____
_____
_____
_____

Definitions:

_____
_____
_____
_____
_____
_____
_____
_____

Cross-Reference Scriptures:

_____
_____
_____
_____
_____
_____
_____
_____

STUDY

What is the text saying to me?

Use the S.P.E.C.K. Method to explore the text.

S.IN TO CONFESS + AVOID

In the passage, does God say something about sin? Is there a sin to confess? Is there a sin that I should avoid?

P.ROMISE TO KEEP

Does God communicate a promise for me to claim?

E.XAMPLE TO FOLLOW

Do I find role models in this passage? What character traits and which actions are commendable? Which are not?

C.OMMAND TO OBEY

Are there any specific commands given for me to follow. What does God want me to apply to my life today and this week so that I develop Godly character and habits?

K. – KNOWLEDGE ABOUT GOD

What does this passage tell me about God or about Jesus Christ or the Holy Spirit? What is God like? What are His attributes? What does He do? What does He like and dislike? What is His attitude?

NOTE - you can't always answer all 5 parts.

STUDY

S. in to confess + avoid

_____
_____
_____
_____
_____
_____
_____

P. romise to keep

_____
_____
_____
_____
_____
_____
_____
_____
_____

E. xample to follow

_____
_____
_____
_____
_____
_____
_____
_____
_____

STUDY

C. ommand to obey

_____
_____
_____
_____
_____
_____
_____
_____
_____
_____
_____
_____

K. nowledge about God

_____
_____
_____
_____
_____
_____
_____
_____
_____
_____
_____
_____
_____
_____
_____
_____
_____

TUNE IN

Relax, let go, be quiet before the Lord and listen.

This is a time of focus. Focus on the scripture and set your mind on the Father, Son, and Holy Spirit. Take as much time as you need. Don't rush this part! After some time has passed, use the space below to write anything God revealed or spoke to you.

_____
_____
_____
_____
_____
_____
_____
_____
_____
_____
_____
_____
_____
_____
_____
_____
_____
_____
_____
_____
_____
_____
_____
_____
_____

LIVE

How can you apply this Word to your life?

Why does what I learned today matter? How do I implement it in my life today? How should my perspective change based on what I have learned? Look for applications that affect your relationship to God, with others, and your view of self. Use the space below to explore these questions.

_____
_____
_____
_____
_____
_____
_____
_____
_____
_____
_____
_____
_____
_____
_____
_____
_____
_____
_____
_____
_____
_____
_____
_____
_____
_____
_____
_____
_____

ENCOURAGE

How I can share what I have learned to help someone else?

When do I plan to share this? Who do I plan to sharing this with? How do I plan to share this? In-person? Text message? Phone call? Social Media? Use the space below to develop a plan of action.

_____
_____
_____
_____
_____
_____
_____
_____
_____
_____
_____
_____
_____
_____
_____
_____
_____
_____
_____
_____
_____
_____
_____
_____
_____
_____
_____
_____

Additional Notes:

_____
_____
_____
_____
_____
_____
_____
_____
_____
_____
_____
_____
_____
_____
_____
_____
_____
_____
_____
_____
_____
_____
_____
_____
_____
_____

How to Study the Bible
The H.U.S.T.L.E. Way

H — **HUMBLE**
Humble yourself and pray.

U — **UNDERSTAND**
Look up different translations, definitions and cross references.

S — **STUDY**
What is the text saying to me?

T — **TUNE IN**
Relax, let go, be quiet before the Lord and listen.

L — **LIVE**
How can you apply this Word to your life?

E — **ENCOURAGE**
How I can share what I have learned to help someone else?

The H.U.S.T.L.E. Bible Study Method

Date:

HUMBLE
yourself and pray.

James 1:5, KJV:
"If any of you lack wisdom, let him ask of God, that giveth to all men liberally, and upbraideth not; and it shall be given him."

Lord, thank You for this time You've given me to open Your Word and discover who You are. Thank You that You don't leave us in the dark about who You are and what You are doing in the world, but that You have revealed Yourself and Your Will through the Bible, Your sacred Words to us.

Lord, I need wisdom as I read Your Word. You promise us in James 1:5 that we only have to ask for wisdom to receive it. Lord, please give me Your wisdom now as I approach Your Word. Help me discern the truth of this text. Help me not rely on my own understanding. Thank you God for the clarity, encouragement and hope Your Word brings.

In Jesus' Name I pray, Amen.

Use the space below to pray specifically about what you would like God to reveal through your Bible Study.

Dear Heavenly Father:

_____
_____
_____
_____
_____
_____
_____
_____
_____
_____
_____
_____
_____
_____
_____
_____
_____
_____
_____
_____
_____
_____
_____
_____
_____

In Jesus Name I pray, Amen

UNDERSTAND
Look up different translations, definitions and cross references.

Scripture: _____

Use the space below to write out the scripture in your favorite translation, then choose another translation to write the scripture out.

Favorite Translation:

_____
_____
_____
_____
_____
_____
_____
_____
_____

Another Translation:

_____
_____
_____
_____
_____
_____
_____
_____
_____

Note any words that are different between the two translations. Use a Bible Dictionary to look up the words. Also read the cross-reference scriptures to dive deeper into the scripture and gain a better understanding.

UNDERSTAND

Words that stand out/are different per translation:

_____
_____
_____
_____
_____
_____
_____
_____

Definitions:

_____
_____
_____
_____
_____
_____
_____
_____

Cross-Reference Scriptures:

_____
_____
_____
_____
_____
_____
_____
_____

STUDY

What is the text saying to me?

Use the S.P.E.C.K. Method to explore the text.

S.IN TO CONFESS + AVOID

In the passage, does God say something about sin? Is there a sin to confess? Is there a sin that I should avoid?

P.ROMISE TO KEEP

Does God communicate a promise for me to claim?

E.XAMPLE TO FOLLOW

Do I find role models in this passage? What character traits and which actions are commendable? Which are not?

C.OMMAND TO OBEY

Are there any specific commands given for me to follow. What does God want me to apply to my life today and this week so that I develop Godly character and habits?

K. – KNOWLEDGE ABOUT GOD

What does this passage tell me about God or about Jesus Christ or the Holy Spirit? What is God like? What are His attributes? What does He do? What does He like and dislike? What is His attitude?

NOTE - you can't always answer all 5 parts.

STUDY

S. in to confess + avoid

_____
_____
_____
_____
_____
_____

P. romise to keep

_____
_____
_____
_____
_____
_____

E. xample to follow

_____
_____
_____
_____
_____
_____
_____

STUDY

C.ommand to obey

_____
_____
_____
_____
_____
_____
_____
_____
_____
_____
_____
_____

K.nowledge about God

_____
_____
_____
_____
_____
_____
_____
_____
_____
_____
_____
_____
_____
_____

TUNE IN

Relax, let go, be quiet before the Lord and listen.

This is a time of focus. Focus on the scripture and set your mind on the Father, Son, and Holy Spirit. Take as much time as you need. Don't rush this part! After some time has passed, use the space below to write anything God revealed or spoke to you.

_____
_____
_____
_____
_____
_____
_____
_____
_____
_____
_____
_____
_____
_____
_____
_____
_____
_____
_____
_____
_____
_____
_____
_____
_____
_____

LIVE

How can you apply this Word to your life?

Why does what I learned today matter? How do I implement it in my life today? How should my perspective change based on what I have learned? Look for applications that affect your relationship to God, with others, and your view of self. Use the space below to explore these questions.

_____
_____
_____
_____
_____
_____
_____
_____
_____
_____
_____
_____
_____
_____
_____
_____
_____
_____
_____
_____
_____
_____
_____
_____

ENCOURAGE

How I can share what I have learned to help someone else?

When do I plan to share this? Who do I plan to sharing this with? How do I plan to share this? In-person? Text message? Phone call? Social Media? Use the space below to develop a plan of action.

_____
_____
_____
_____
_____
_____
_____
_____
_____
_____
_____
_____
_____
_____
_____
_____
_____
_____
_____
_____
_____
_____
_____
_____
_____
_____
_____
_____
_____

Additional Notes:

"The Bible contains all the extant revelations of God, which He designed to be the rule of faith and practice for his Church; so that nothing can rightfully be imposed on the consciences of men as truth or duty which is not taught directly or by necessary implication in the Holy Scriptures."

Charles Hodge

The H.U.S.T.L.E. Bible Study Method

About the Creator

LaKesha L. Williams, acclaimed author, speaker and minister of the Gospel of Jesus Christ, was born to parents Doris & Cleo Williams in Raleigh, North Carolina in 1983. To know LaKesha is to experience a calming spirit infused with gut-wrenching laughter at unexpected times. She has a passion for giving, which is demonstrated wholeheartedly through her founding of Born Overcomers Inc., a needs-based, nonprofit organization and movement dedicated to promoting the belief that we were all Born to Overcome.

She has authored more than nine books, including three bestsellers; and is also a featured co-author in Open Your G.I.F.T.S. presented by actress & comedian Kim Coles. She is also the Owner of The Vision to Fruition Group, LLC, a consulting firm dedicated to helping others bring their visions to fruition. In 2015, LaKesha received the Sistas Inspiring Sistas Phenomenal Woman Award, and is the 2016 Indie Author Legacy Award Recipient in the Author on the Rise category; a 2016 Metro Phenomenal Woman Honoree; a 2017 TDK Publishing Author of the Year nominee; and the 2018 iShine Awards winner for Author of the Year. LaKesha is currently a student at Capital Bible Seminary pursuing a Masters Degree in Christian Care.

LaKesha, is a virgin and an advocate of abstinence, purity and virginity until marriage. Currently, LaKesha resides in Maryland and enjoys serving in the community, fellowshipping with her church family at The Remnant of Hope International Church in Prince Frederick Maryland (under the leadership of Pastor Margo Gross), and spending time with her family and friends, watching movies, sharing stories and creating new memories.

Connect with LaKesha

Web:
www.vision-fruition.com
www.vtfpublishing.com
www.vtfprintshop.com
www.coachkesha.com
www.bornovercomers.com
www.hustlegodsway.com

Phone:
240-343-3563

Facebook Pages:
Born Overcomers Inc.
The Vision to Fruition Group
The Vision to Fruition Publishing House
The VTF Print Shop
Coach Kesha
Hustle God's Way

Personal Facebook:
www.facebook.com/lakesha.williams
Instragram & Twitter: @iamcoachkesha

www.ingramcontent.com/pod-product-compliance
Lightning Source LLC
Chambersburg PA
CBHW080358170426
43193CB00016B/2759